EXPlicit
EXPectations

THE ESSENTIAL GUIDE & TOOLKIT OF
MANAGEMENT FUNDAMENTALS

R. KARL HEBENSTREIT, PH.D., PCC

Front Cover picture by R. Karl Hebenstreit, Ph.D., PCC
Front and Back Cover Designs by Charlyn Samson

Copyright 2024
Published by Perform & Function, LLC

CONTENTS

"The author delivers exactly what he promises in the title of this book. This is a "must have" for anyone new to the world of leadership. There are indeed countless books on that topic. Karl must have read them all because he synthesizes all his learnings to deliver the essentials to his readers. And he adds his own twist to make this a resource that can be returned to again and again. If you are looking for an up-to-date storehouse of helpful outlines, guides and well tested suggestions that will make your job as a new leader easier, this is a great find! It comes from someone who has been there and done that….and remembers the lessons he has learned."

Dr. Bev Kaye, co-author of *Love 'Em or Lose 'Em, Hello Stay Interviews, Goodbye Talent Loss, Up Is Not the Only Way, Help Them Grow or Watch Them Go*

"Explicit Expectations: The Essential Guide & Toolkit of Management Fundamentals offers a groundbreaking perspective on human interaction and leadership. This book is a roadmap to becoming the kind of leader others aspire to follow, one who leads with empathy, insight, and an unwavering commitment to understanding. *Explicit Expectations* is not just a book; it's a guide to unlocking the full potential of human connection and leadership."

Rebecca Ahmed, Founder & Chief Energy Officer (CEO) of Energetic Impact, Author of *The Energy of Success*

Explicit Expectations is an essential read for any new or aspiring manager, and a great refresher for those with management experience. This comprehensive guide provides a clear and actionable framework for setting and communicating expectations with your team.

Karl's practical advice and real-world examples make it easy to implement effective management practices from day one. From clarifying goals and expectations to providing constructive feedback, this book equips new managers with the tools they need to lead their teams to success.

Whether you're stepping into your first management role or looking to fine-tune your management skills, *Explicit Expectations* is a must-have resource. It will transform the way you approach people management and help you cultivate a high-performing, engaged workforce. I highly recommend this book to any new manager aiming to establish a strong foundation for effective team leadership.

> Kathi Enderes, Ph.D., SVP Research and Global
> Industry Analyst, The Josh Bersin Company

"An invaluable resource for both novice and seasoned managers alike, this book offers practical wisdom in a clear, accessible manner. Its well-crafted structure ensures easy navigation and quick reference, while its insights are immediately applicable in real-world scenarios. Whether you are stepping into a managerial role for the first time or seeking to enhance your leadership skills, this book is a must-have companion on your journey to success."

> Joel Daurity, MBA, President & COO,
> Pattison Sign Group, US

"*Explicit Expectations* is a wonderful, practical, comprehensive, instructional, and supportive playbook for new leaders. There's a ton of great content for experienced leaders, too. The reflection prompts with each chapter facilitate a connection with the reader and the content. The deeper dives are also fantastic. Karl has created a really solid, deep bibliography, which is also really helpful."

> Elizabeth Perusse,
> multi-industry HR practitioner for over 30 years

ACKNOWLEDGEMENTS AND INTRODUCTION

This book is the culmination of my graduate (Human Resource Management) and post-graduate (Organizational Psychology) studies, complemented by over 30 years of corporate experience in the Human Resources and Organization Development departments of some really progressive and caring organizations. I have learned myriad important lessons along the way from some very talented leaders and coworkers. I have seen and experienced challenging and sensitive situations handled very well, and others not as effectively. Reflecting on what I've experienced and learned, I'm indebted to the exemplary leadership of Nancy Vander Zwan at Merck, Janet Konopka at AT&T, Corrine Root at Cushman & Wakefield, Cheryl Kulacz at EMC, Rich Elderkin at Bio-Rad, and Rachael Allison at Genentech. From a personal perspective, I am grateful for the continuous and on-going support and encouragement of my parents (James and Domna), friends, colleagues-turned-friends, my partner Alex, and our three-dog fur family of Chase, Emmett, and Turbo. And a special shout out to Aimee Einstein, whose business need, vision, and support inspired me to create this resource and put it out into the world!

The Why

To paraphrase Charles Dickens's famous opening line of *A Tale of Two Cities*, "It is the best of times (congratulations on being a manager!), it is the most demanding and confusing of times (you're also operating in a brand new world with vastly different requirements, responsibilities, and expectations of you)." This resource is titled "Explicit Expectations" for a very important reason. Not knowing what is expected of you – whether you're a leader or an individual contributor – is the root cause of confusion, disappointment, disengagement, and failure in organizations. It is most effectively countered through focus on strategy, clear goals, communication, and the dispelling of the most harmful of all myths – the Golden Rule. Remember being taught – via myriad vehicles like religion, school, parents, even television commercials for hotel chains – that you should treat others the way YOU want to be treated? What if I were to tell you that this is the mindset that yields misunderstandings (including conflicts and wars), closed-minded thinking, bias, prejudice, discrimination, and self-centered arrogance? The Golden Rule would be 100% effective in a world where everyone is the same and wants to be treated the same way, has the same values, same preferences, same likes/dislikes, same perspectives, same history, same abilities, same ideological thinking, same religious affiliation, etc. Unless you've been living a very sheltered life, without access to any other people, cultures, social media, or news, you logically, intellectually, and realistically know that this is not true. By treating everyone the way we want to be treated ourselves, we are saying that everyone else wants to be treated the same way we do. We are only looking inwardly at ourselves, at the one piece of the puzzle we have, and not outwardly to discover and consider different perspectives and ways of being, and collecting and learning from the rest of the puzzle pieces. At worst, we are holding our views, values, and beliefs paramount as better and more important than others'. We are discounting others' perspectives, needs, and experiences, and devaluing their experiences and existence. And they know, can see, and can feel it. And it doesn't feel good to them.

The How

Instead, to truly understand others' needs, motivations, and expectations, I invite you to consider applying the wisdom of the Platinum Rule: Treat others the way *THEY* want to be treated (as long as it conforms with universal values of not being illegal or causing harm to themselves or others). Engage with others with genuine curiosity to find out what's important to them, what their values, aspirations, motivations, strengths, interests, challenges, fears, and goals are; start collecting the other pieces of the puzzle you don't already have. Doing so with your team members will help you better understand each of them, and know how best to support, manage, and lead them – so that they can use you as the example of the best manager/leader they've ever had (this will make even more sense after you read the next section about your new role). We fall into the Golden Rule trap when we assume we know what others want without actually asking them (this is painfully true in succession planning exercises when managers offer up their team members for roles without first discussing their aspirations with them). We are not mindreaders. As such, we need to have regular conversations with our team members to understand and gain clarity on all the areas around which we are making assumptions that they mimic our own situation. Spoiler alert: They don't.

Once you've managed to challenge the Golden Rule and replace it with the Platinum Rule, I invite you to go one step even further: The Rhodium Rule invites you to take the Platinum Rule insights, learnings, and new puzzle pieces (the differences between your perspectives and others') and integrate them into your own for a more robust comprehension and experience of reality – you are piecing together the bigger puzzle! This is *"AND"* thinking. It's not this OR that; both – and more! – realities can coexist simultaneously and provide a much broader, more strategic view of the world. This will help with your evolution from myopic and tactical to broader, more strategic thinking, as well. Integrating *"AND"* thinking opens up our minds to more complexity and greater understanding. Try it! It really works! And just wait until you see, experience, and learn from the entire and complete puzzle picture!

Your (New) Role

Think about the best/your favorite manager, leader, sports coach, teacher or role model you've ever had. How would you describe them? Why are they the best/your favorite? What makes them stand out above all the others? What criteria are you using to differentiate them from all the others? How did they make you feel? What did you learn from them? What was their impact on you?

When people are asked this question, the responses typically include "firm, but fair" along with variations on being supportive, visionary/inspirational, having their backs, and a slew of other attributes associated with emotional intelligence and social skills (self-awareness, patience, empathy, etc.). Technical skills rarely make the cut. As you will see with each of the areas you are (now) tasked with, emotional intelligence is the differentiator.

You are about to (or already have) embark(ed) on a very influential journey that will impact the lives, livelihoods, happiness, and careers of those the organization has entrusted to report to you. This is a big deal. And its successful execution is totally possible ... when you choose to focus on some fundamentals that I have aggregated based on my experiences:

THE SEVEN CS OF EXPLICIT EXPECTATIONS

- Clarity – The greatest impact you can make on your organization and your people is to provide as much clarity and direction (but not micro-managing directions) as possible. The need for clarity will be intensified in times of decision-making, when your team will count on you to make prompt and timely decisions to be acted upon. You and your team members will encounter a lot of organizational noise, including competing priorities, distractions, competition, external demands, socio-political intrusions, etc. Through it all, it's up to you to remind yourself and your team of where to focus your efforts. Use the organization's mission and your team's goals as a true north to help identify and reinforce which activities should be engaged in and which can be deferred, delegated, or dismissed. We'll dive deeper into how to do that in Chapter 7.
- Consistency & Confidence – Your team will look for you for stability in times of chaos and disruption. How can and will you show up as a stable, consistent, confident, reliable rock in the midst of volatility, uncertainty, com-

plexity, and ambiguity (VUCA)? The concept of equity is closely related to this – how will you ensure that your team members are and feel treated equitably. We can look to the Platinum Rule to help us understand the difference between Equity and Fairness. Not everyone wants to or needs to be treated the same way. Some people will require more attention, others less. Different leadership styles will need to be used with different teammates at different times. The consistency comes in the form of team members feeling that they are supported in a way that they need and that you are there for them when and in the way they need you to be; that everyone has access to you when they need you and in the way they need you to show up for them, without any perceived favoritism. The confidence comes into play when you show strength in making fair and equitable decisions to lead, support, and grow them.

- Communication – Whenever employee engagement/satisfaction surveys are conducted, the top gripe employees have is that they feel that their leaders don't communicate enough or honestly enough with them. When this happens, the rumor mill goes rampant, trust erodes, productivity declines, and disengagement soars. Your role is to communicate openly, honestly, and frequently – and to follow through when you need to find out more details. Consistency comes into play here, as well, since the communication has to be consistent with the organizational messages and what other managers and leaders are saying. There will be times when you won't be able to reveal certain information you know in advance – in those cases, it is best to say that you aren't at liberty to say anything at this point, and that you will as soon as you can (and do so then).

- Collaboration – We live in a society and work in organizations and with systems that reward individuality. We also have learned that better, more innovative solutions, products, and services are created when people work and share together. Your role is to create and foster the most effective and conducive environment for this to occur – where diverse perspectives are invited, considered, and acted upon, failures are learned from, and everyone feels welcomed, treated, and rewarded as an equal.

- Compassion – Your team will look to you to show that you understand and empathize with what they're going through – whether it's internal company politics, obstacles to meeting their goals, personal issues, or in delivering unpleasant news. Before jumping to solutioning or logical problem-solving mode – which is so tempting to do, and may be easier than staying with feelings – take a moment to "sit with" your team member, ask them questions with genuine curiosity to better understand, acknowledge their situation, truly picture and put yourself in their shoes, and ask them what they need. Is it just venting? Are they ready for co-creating a solution? Is it advice? Referral to the Employee Assistance Program? Other resources? Time to think/process on their own? Time off? Something else? Show them you care without diminishing their situation or making it about you. Ask them, "How can I help?" Follow up with them to see how they're doing, if the issue is resolved, and if they need anything else that you can do.

- Coaching – The evolution to managers as coaches is real and here. One of your greatest legacies as a manager and leader will be the development of your team members. Developing your own coaching style – in addition to other styles you will also use, situationally – will be critical in making this happen. More on this in Chapter 8.

The aforementioned "Seven Cs of Explicit Expectations" come into play in the five practices that effective leaders bring to life:

- **Inspire a Shared Vision**, including your organization's mission and values.
- **Model the Way**, especially role modeling your organization's values and ensuring everyone is treated consistently and equitably.

- **Challenge the Process** to bring forth creativity and better ways of doing things.
- **Connect with and get to know your people** via 1:1s, to understand their aspirations and interests, motivations, challenges, etc., applying the Platinum Rule (treat others the way *they* want to be treated, with the caveats previously discussed) instead of assuming that everyone aspires to and likes the same things we do. Empathize with them.
- **Enable Others to Act** through ensuring their people's understanding of their role's expectations and how their roles connect to our mission and goals, coaching them to success, developing them to their interest and potential, removing obstacles, etc.

 For a deeper dive on these five practices, check out the source work of Kouzes and Posner (see the *Sources & Additional Resources* section).

The What

So … welcome to a compilation of the most powerful tools proven to help leaders optimize their effectiveness in their people management roles!

We will approach each topic from three perspectives:

- Self – what are your experiences, needs, and resulting expectations around this? What's your relationship to the topic?
- Team – what does each team member need and expect from you in this regard? How is each team member's needs and experiences different and what are those implications on how you manage and support them individually and as a team?

- Organization – what are the organization's expectations in this regard? What is being attempted to be accomplished through this means? What does this mean to/for you?

We will conclude each topic with a Reality Check – how does this actually work in *your* experience within *your* organization. And how does this align with your values, needs, and expectations? Regardless of what stated expectations exist, who and what behaviors are being rewarded at the highest levels? Is there alignment between stated expectations and rewarded behavior? What does this mean for you?

Ultimately, you will incorporate all of your learnings, reminders, and take-aways from each chapter and fill out the "Explicit Expectations Engagement & Alignment Guide" with each of your team members … AND with your own leader! Co-creating and completing this as close to the start of your work relationship – and then reviewing it at least quarterly to see if any updates or changes are warranted – is the key to ensuring that you and your team members are and stay aligned in what you expect from each other. This will serve to prevent and avoid any unpleasant surprises, disappointments, or frustrations that inevitably lead to dissatisfaction, disengagement, poor performance, and turnover. And this will contribute to optimizing your management and leadership effectiveness, so that you make the list of best leaders when your team members are asked this question.

SPECIAL NOTE

This guide/toolkit is not meant to and does not replace nor does it supersede any of your organization's Human Resources/ People & Culture policies and practices. It is meant to provide a foundational basis and understanding of – and complement to – your organization's existing guidelines and policies. Your success as a people manager depends on your on-going partnership with your Human Resources/People & Culture Business Partner, your manager, and other key stakeholders in your organization.

CHAPTER 1

STRATEGIC PLANNING & ORGANIZATIONAL DESIGN

One of the key roles of a manager is to ensure that their teams know the direction where they're heading and why what they're doing is important to the success of the organization and its mission.

Simon Sinek talks about the importance of "Starting with Why." That is part of an organization's mission – why the organization exists. Marrying this to the vision (the ultimate, aspirational end state) creates a very powerful, compelling, and motivating tool to guide the organization and its employees. It's the clarity and direction that supersedes everything else in times of chaos and confusion. A truly compelling, meaningful, and widely-held vision and mission serve to ignite creativity, innovation, performance, and results.

As a people-leader, the Vision and Mission of the organization are very powerful tools available for your use in energizing, motivating, and guiding your team. Referencing the Vision and Mission of the organization helps:

- reground you and your team in times of chaos
- provide clarity and direction for next steps forward, and
- remind yourselves of your connection to the organization and reason for being here and doing the important work you're doing to create the impact you're making.

All goals (to be discussed in Chapter 5) will be created to support and feed into the mission.

Though not required or mandated, creating a sub-mission for your team (if necessary for additional clarity) may help to show and remind your team members how the work your team/function/department is doing contributes to the overall mission of your organization. If your organization hasn't already created one, and/or if you decide to do this for your team, you may find the following structure helpful in getting started and focused:

> *The _____ team exists to deliver (describe product/services) by (describe/list 3-5 major activities performed to create products/services; consider incorporating our values). We do this so that/because (describe purpose of meeting customers' needs/tie into your organization's mission, if it already exists).*

Note that it is probably NOT necessary for you to create a vision for your team, as your organization's vision can serve as that ultimate, aspirational end state to which your team is contributing.

Your organization's Strategic Plan will include:

- Mission, Vision, and Values
- Overall organizational Goals and Objectives
- Key initiatives
- SWOT (Strengths, Weaknesses, Opportunities, Threats) analysis, including highlighting the unique value the organization provides, and the competitive environment in which you're operating
- Action plans and tactics
- Resource allocation
- Identification of stakeholders, competitors.

Taken holistically, it will serve to inform all that you do, including your organizational structure, workforce planning, goal-setting, performance management, budgeting, etc.

Speaking of organizational structure, let's visit the "STAR" model developed by Jay R. Galbraith in 1977, and still in use today because of its powerful insights and continued relevance:

1. Strategy – it all starts with the organization's strategy and direction. Why are we all here working together? Towards what end goal? For whom?
2. Structure – Once the strategy is understood, the form of the organization can take place. How will we achieve the goals set forth in the strategy? What structure can best set us up for success? Centralized, with Centers of Excellence? Decentralized, with laser focus on customer and stakeholder needs and customized service? A hybrid of both? How does this impact for accountability and scope of authority?
3. Processes – Once the best structure for the organization's strategy and customer needs is identified, gaps will inevitably show up – there is no perfect structure that addresses all issues. The gaps will be filled through new processes, driving the sharing of information throughout the organization to the appropriate groups that need it to achieve the organization's goals in support of its strategy.
4. Rewards – As we will see in Chapter 11, rewards are a very necessary consideration to ensure that the workforce's intrinsic and extrinsic motivational needs are being met. Since you don't yet know who these employees are – and since turnover and growth will require the addition of new employees at some point – a rewards system that is likely to appeal to the whole population needs to be considered, developed, and implemented.
5. People – Now that all of our preparations have been made about why and how we will do the work, we can focus on

the resources who are going to actually do the work – the people – and the policies that will provide guardrails and guidelines for them to do it. Note that the people component is the last step of this process. Organizations make decisions about the structure of the organization based on business strategies and needs. Hiring decisions are also based on the organization's business strategies and needs. Organizational structures are not built around people or roles. An assessment of employee – or candidate – capabilities to meet the needs of the organization's strategy results in their placement into roles the organization needs to execute on its strategy and achieve its goals.

 For a deeper dive, check out Jay Galbraith's source work (see the *Sources & Additional Resources* section).

We would be sorely remiss if we didn't address diversity here, as an integral part of this process. In order for any organization to guarantee that it will successfully and innovatively meet the needs of its diverse stakeholders, it must work to ensure that processes exist to attract, retain, and motivate people from diverse backgrounds, with diverse experiences, and diverse perspectives that mirror the diversity of their customer base … and that they are invited, valued, respected, heard, and acted upon. Only then will it successfully prevent groupthink (that has resulted in so many devastating catastrophes and preventable failures) and truly optimize the brainpower and talents of its people to create innovative, relevant, timely products, services, and solutions that fuel successful organizations. Also, the operationalization of diversity will be different for each company based on the geography/region of location and service delivery, culture, and history. Let's explore this more in Chapter 2.

SELF: What are your expectations around contributing to your organization's Strategic Plan and organization design? What is your role in Strategic Planning? What is your role in Organization Design? How clear are you about your organization's vision, mission, and goals? How can you use this to create more clarity for yourself, your role, and your team? How can these be made more explicit? What can and will you do about this?

 TEAM: What are your team members' expectations and needs from you and the organization around Strategic Planning? What is your game plan to ensure that your team is aware of and committed to your organization's and team's strategy and use it accordingly to help them in performing their daily duties and guide their decision-making and long-term planning? How can these be made more explicit? What can and will you do about this?

 ORGANIZATION: What are your organization's expectations about your role in Strategic Planning? Who does your organization identify as and reward for being strategic? What is it they do? How can and will you gain more insight into their work and explore their support/mentoring of you in this area? How can these be made more explicit? What can and will you do to become a bigger player in this arena?

REALITY CHECK: How well does your organization do Strategic Planning? How aligned are your organization's decisions and actions to the stated vision, mission, values, and goals? How does your organization's strategic plan inform the organizational structure? Does it center around business and strategic needs or are structures built around specific people? Does it work/is it effective? Is diversity part of the strategic plan and leveraged in the structure? What can and will you do and how can you influence this to be even better?

CHAPTER 2

JUSTICE, EQUITY, DIVERSITY, & INCLUSION CONSIDERATIONS

To ensure that we are creating a psychologically-safe environment, where all of our organization's team members can bring their whole selves to work and contribute their diverse perspectives without fear of reprisal, consider these insights:

TOP 10 BEST PRACTICES TO CREATE A PSYCHOLOGICALLY-SAFE WORK ENVIRONMENT

1. Effective Communications, based on good guidance on how to do so – set clear norms and guidance around communication (i.e., "What we need from each other in team meetings …"), "User Manuals" on shared drives for each teammate
2. Use Inclusive Language (acknowledge differences and past history/harm, changes over time and across individuals, requires humility) – i.e., don't use "historically underrepresented" (since this is the current situation as well); Check out www.consciousstyleguide.com for a free online inclusive language tool
   - Diverse Group/Org/Team (instead of "Diverse" individual/candidate)
   - Use specifics whenever possible instead of "People of Color" – specify what you're focusing on!
     o "Marginalized/underserved" instead of "minority"

6

- ○ "Black people, white people," etc. instead of "the Blacks, the Asians" (don't use an adjective as a noun)
- ○ "Safe/approved/allow list" and "block/deny list" instead of "Black List" or "White List"
- ○ Remove "Hey Guys" from your vocabulary; instead, use "All" or "Everyone"

3. Name and Attribute Sources of Information/Contribution, saying and spelling their names correctly (to give credit for what they bring to the party)
   - Peoples' names brought up by others is a way to show how influential people are and leads to promotions
   - Saying someone else's name is personal and inclusionary
   - Correct coworkers who mispronounce colleagues' names

4. Amplify Others – the public endorsement of someone's idea or contribution with proper attribution of credit
   - The amplifier makes the amplified seem more influential, and themselves look good as well, and can help underrepresented voices be heard
   - Teams that use amplification build stronger connections and more psychological safety
   - Personally recommend their work/ideas to others especially to those in leadership, show public/private gratitude in various ways, increase their visibility with others

5. Be an Upstander, not a Bystander! Interrupt, Intervene and Follow Up!
   - "Wow, I'm really surprised to hear you say that!" to give others an out to correct what they just did/said (microaggressions, etc.)
   - "Thanks, I've actually been looking for a chance to correct that misconception …"
   - "Oops!"
   - "That's not OK/how we do things here/language we use here."

- "Ouch!"
- "Are people still using that word/phrase?"

6. Use Inclusive Symbols and Imagery to communicate what kind of organization you are – and don't wait until the last minute to honor someone for their lived experience.
    - Download a free diversity calendar (Search "Current Year Diversity Calendar")
    - Check out www.betterallies.com/photos for free diverse and inclusive images

7. Include those impacted on/with/by a decision/initiative/ program – don't assume you know what's best for others without including them
    - Builds rapport
    - Gets to surface own unknowns
    - Increases buy-in
    - Avoids consensus rush leading to bad/insensitive decisions/outputs

8. Focus on Accountability (individual and collective owner-ship for any issue, the glue that ties commitment to results.
    - What is each employee's personal responsibility for promoting inclusion at work?
    - What policies, practices, or procedures need to be for-malized to ensure accountability?
        ○ Use visible pledges/commitments on employee badges/ID cards, etc.
        ○ Find an accountability partner and hold each other accountable to make inclusion a priority

9. Use and Encourage Positive Micro-Acts – micro-affirma-tions, micro-inclusions, and micro-allyship
    - "Opening doors" of opportunity to others; invite them to participate in a meeting, expose to leadership, co-present a training, collaboration, cross-training
    - Show inclusion and caring – find out more about what's going on for them outside of work to see them as themselves.

- Listen to them – invite them to speak/contribute first in a meeting
- Give kudos – check in with them to see what it takes for them to be seen and heard in the organization
- Identify and provide needed resources – connect personal life to work
- Share knowledge – communicate the same information and messages to everyone

10. Model vulnerability so that people feel that it's less risky to be who they are
    - Admit what you don't know and ask for help when you need it
    - Make it safe to take risks, to fail, and to learn
    - Share stories
    - Focus on the learning, not just the outcomes
    - Take accountability when things go wrong

 For a deeper dive and more information about this topic, check out Tara B. Taylor's source work at www. adrvantage.com.

Remember that, as human beings, we are all subject to implicit bias that is inherent to our upbringing and socialization. It is best to be self-aware about these and do what we can to minimize or prevent them as much as possible.

IMPLICIT HUMAN BIASES

Primacy / Recency	Evaluating on the first or most recent subjective impression or perception (positive or negative) of someone based on things they have done.
Halo / Horn	Basing all aspects of an individual's performance on a general subjective impression, favorable or unfavorable, that originates from only one aspect of their performance.
Familiarity / Similar-to-me	Evaluating an individual more favorably because they possess characteristics similar to your own.
Negativity	Focusing on, considering, and weighing negative behavior or poor performance more heavily than positive performance.
Attributions | Fundamental Attribution Error	Attributing a specific cause, reason, or motive to an individual's behavior, which may or may not be the actual cause of the behavior.
Strictness	Evaluating everyone overly strictly because "managers should be tough graders" and "nobody is perfect."

TO REDUCE/MITIGATE IMPLICIT BIASES:

Challenge Yourself!

In the same way as challenging others, you can challenge your own unconscious assumptions and biases. If you notice yourself making an assumption without the evidence to support it, remember to ask yourself the following questions:

- Is this really true?
- What objective evidence do I have?
- Is this thought based on objective facts?
- What is the impact of this assumption on me? What does this say about me?
- How would I feel if someone made these assumptions about me?

When (and it is a when, not an if) we find that our biases may have unconsciously and unintentionally caused harm, we can turn to the DARE Model for a way to navigate and learn from the situation.

THE DARE MODEL (Dethra U. Giles)

When you find yourself needing to engage in a challenging or sensitive conversation that may involve bias – and you want to make sure that you resolve it and not make it potentially worse – turn to Dethra Giles's DARE Model for guidance:

Describe: facts not interpretation (our minds jump to interpretation first – the brain is a blind organ – it will fill in meaning (filled in with your life's lens and biases) to what it sees. So, stay in description phase as long as possible.

- Description: the facts (different from our own Truths, how we've interpreted an objective fact to make it describe us relatively). Ask clarifying questions to get more facts.
- Interpretation: what you make the facts mean

Acknowledge: Recognize, not minimize. Acknowledge similarities without minimizing differences. "I don't see color" minimizes others' experiences.

Review: Narrative, not bias. Review and question the narratives that we have accepted as fact. Review and question historical context, school, family, our organizations, etc. Family narratives are much more ingrained than education system ones.

Biases often inform what we have accepted as fact. What seems like a harmless generalization on the surface can reveal what we believe about a group of people at a deeper level and negatively impact individuals of that group, even when it seems positive. "I assume you are making an intentional decision to not acknowledge."

Engage: Understanding, not Conversion. The hardest component/ step since this is external, not internal like the other preceding steps.

Engage in a conversation (and experience a person) for understanding, not conversion. You can agree and not align. Alignment says I understand where you're coming from (this is what you were taught), even if I don't agree.

DO:

- Listen, with the intent to truly understand
- Say "Can we pause to process?" or "Let's pause and come back to continue this conversation at a later time when we are better able to do so."
- Begin to unfold the narrative

DON'T:

- Prepare an argument in your head to respond
- Interrupt (this results in the other shutting down or elevating)
- Become defensive (resist this natural response to someone telling you that you're wrong)
- Behave or react out of defensiveness (instead, monitor our judgment and don't act on it)
- Assume and jump to interpretations (which are probably not fully-informed or right)

When you mistakenly say something unintended and offensive (and you will):

- Don't let a misstep stop the conversation
- Own your mistakes
- Ask for clarification
- Inquire of ways to correct the offense (and prevent future occurrences)
- Be thankful

- Apply the learning to future conversations

Otherwise, the offended party/parties will think it was intentional.

For a deeper dive on this and more, check out Dethra U. Giles's source work at dethragiles.org.

SELF: What are your implicit biases (don't worry, everyone has them!)? What are you doing to overcome and mitigate them? How do you keep yourself open to other, differing perspectives? What have you learned from broadening your horizons? What are you doing to ensure you're being as inclusive as possible and creating a psychologically-safe environment for everyone to be able to bring their authentic selves to the team and to the organization? What benefits have you seen of doing this? What more can and will you do about this?

TEAM: How aware are each of your team members about their implicit biases? How diverse is your team? How do they navigate and leverage diversity within the team and in their interactions? How safe do they feel to speak up with their own diverse perspectives and experiences? How do they treat and respond to other teammates when they speak up with a diverse perspective or opinion? What are your explicit expectations of them in the arena of Justice, Equity, Diversity, and Inclusion? What are their explicit expectations of you in this area? What can and will you do to help your team improve in this area?

ORGANIZATION: What are your organization's explicit expectations of your role in supporting Justice, Equity, Diversity, and Inclusion? Are there corporate goals and report-outs around this? Is there a Chief Diversity Officer or department where this is a focus and through which resources, guidance, and support are available? What can and will you do to help your organization improve in this area?

REALITY CHECK: How does your organization fare when it comes to Justice, Equity, Diversity, and Inclusion? What are the optics around this? When you look at your Board of Directors and your Executive Leadership Team, how diverse is that picture? Do you see people who resemble you in that mix? What does that tell you? How easy is it for you to hire diverse talent? How long is their typical tenure compared to the average for your organization? Why is that? Are there Employee Resource/Affinity Groups that are sanctioned by your organization? What are they used for? Social get-togethers? Awareness programs? Partnering with business in recruiting and retention/engagement initiatives? What can and will you do to make a positive difference and impact in this area?

CHAPTER 3

RECRUITING, INTERVIEWING, & HIRING

Recruiting is a two-way street. Just as you interview candidates to assess their culture and technical fit within your organization and team, candidates are also interviewing you as a boss/team/company for whom they would want to come work. As such, it is imperative to always best represent yourself and your organization by:

- scheduling and interviewing candidates in an expedient manner
- showing up on time for your interviews; not having the candidate wait
- being prepared by reviewing the candidate's résumé, job description, and questions you will ask in advance
- casting the organization in the best possible light
- living/showcasing the organization's values

To ensure a timely experience for both candidate and organization:

- Hiring managers and interviewers commit to responding to recruiter submissions of candidate résumés to be interviewed within 24 hours
- Hiring managers and interviewers commit to holding a candidate review meeting within 24 hours of the final interview of all candidates for the open role

The Candidate Guide that follows provides a wide range of behavioral questions that you can ask to assess a candidate's fit within your organization. Behavioral interviews are based on the premise that a person's past behavior is the best indicator and predictor of their future behavior in similar circumstances. Behavioral questions ("What did you do when …") are a better predictor of a candidate's likely performance than theoretical questions ("What would you do if …"), which may have clear, socially-accepted answers, but may never play out that way for a particular candidate. The more details you can extract from the candidate to answer each question, the better idea you will have about their actual knowledge of, experience with, and behavior in these types of situations. Behavioral questions are more often used to identify fit with values and you can use them for technical skills evaluations as well. Once you have received the answer to the question (usually in the "STAR" framework of Situation, Task, Actions taken by the candidate, hopefully-positive Result or lesson learned and reapplied in a future situation), use the rubric in the right-hand column to assign a score as to how well the candidate performed in that area. In cases of multiple interviewers of the same candidate, arrange and decide in advance who will ask which questions – perhaps even from different categories, as time permits – so the candidate isn't asked the same question by every interviewer. Feel free to choose only one question per category, whichever makes the most sense for the role. If the candidate is having a difficult time answering that question, you may select a different one from the same category, reminding the candidate that past work examples are preferable, but academic experiences or other organizational experiences may provide good examples as well (the caveat being that some hobbies/pastimes may broach protected territory – see the list of permissible versus illegal/actionable questions at the end).

CANDIDATE INTERVIEW GUIDE
– HIRING MANAGER

Introduction/Opening/Sell – 5 - 10 minutes

- Introduce yourself
- Ensure the candidate's comfort (water, restroom break?)
- Talk about your role, how long you've worked here and in which capacities, and your role in the interview process (hiring manager, peer, key customer, stakeholder, etc.)
- Talk about our mission and your department's charter/ goals

Hiring Manager Deep Dive: 1 – 2 hours

Walk the candidate through their résumé and ask each of these questions about every job, in chronological order (oldest to most recent). If there are more than 5-10 jobs you can group them (functionally, by industry, etc.).

- *What were you hired to do?*
- *What accomplishments are you most proud of?*
- *What were some low points during that job?*
- *What was your boss's name (how do you spell it?) What will they say about you when I call them during my reference checks?*
- *Who was on the team you inherited/who were your peers (as appropriate)? What were the team dynamics like (performance, collaboration, etc.)? How would they describe you as a team leader/teammate?*
- *Why did you leave that job?*

Close – 10 – 15 minutes

- Ask the candidate: *"What questions do you have?"* and answer them to the best of your ability
- Explain the next steps in the recruitment process
- Thank the candidate for coming

Post-Selection

- Work with Recruitment to make offer to successful candidate
- Work with Recruitment to disposition and notify unselected candidates, with appropriate feedback for the candidates, should they inquire
- Start On-Boarding preparations (see Chapter 4)

CANDIDATE INTERVIEW
GUIDE - INTERVIEWERS

Introduction/Opening/Sell – 10% of scheduled interview time

- Introduce yourself
- Ensure the candidate's comfort (water, restroom break?)
- Talk about your role, how long you've worked here and in which capacities, and your role in the interview process (hiring manager, peer, key customer, stakeholder, etc.)
- Talk about our mission and your department's charter/goals

Candidate Résumé Review – 10% of scheduled interview time

Walk the candidate through their resume and clarify any areas of confusion/concern (technical and/or functional)

Structured/Behavioral Interview – 70% of scheduled interview time

Ask the predetermined/pre-assigned behavioral and skill-related questions you will need to provide your proper assessment of the candidate. Ask all of your candidates for this role the same job-related questions to mitigate potential bias. Explain that you would like the candidate to answer each question by telling you the specific Situation, Hindrance/Task, Actions that they took, the Result of those Actions, and then an Evaluation of their approach (did it work, have they approached this type of situation differently since then, etc.). Suggested areas are (see following pages for example questions for each area):

- Organization's Values
- Technical/Functional Skills

Close – 10% of scheduled interview time

- Ask the candidate: "*What questions do you have?*" and answer them to the best of your ability. It's OK to deflect appropriate questions to the Hiring Manager or Recruiter (i.e., compensation, benefits)
- Explain the next steps in the recruitment process
- Thank the candidate for coming

Interviewer's Next Steps:

- Complete your notes and evaluations on the candidate (see last page), assigning appropriate ratings per competency
- Meet with the rest of the members of the interview team and provide your feedback and recommendations

BEHAVIORAL QUESTIONS	RATING SCALE
1. Tell me about a situation where you had to quickly adjust to a change in your organization that required you and your team to shift priorities. How did this change affect you? 2. Tell me about a time that you had to adapt to a difficult situation. 3. Give me an example of a situation that required you to change your work style/approach to meet a certain objective or to get people to respond more favorably. 4. Think of a situation in which information, instructions or objectives were ambiguous. Describe what you did to clarify the situation. How people deal with their own failures at work is largely impacted by how they think the organization will deal with those failures. 5. Due to the continuous flow of internal and external customer projects, in this position you will need to adapt to shifting priorities. 6. Describe something you've done that shows you would be good at that. 7. Tell me about a time when you did a good job of maintaining high productivity in a stressful situation. 8. Think of a situation in which you dealt positively with a change that affected your job requirements.	5: Evidence of having a high tolerance for change. Ability to shift gears to meet business objectives. Was able to positively deal with changes that affect job requirements; adapt to shifting priorities in response to the needs of internal and external clients; quickly recognize situations / conditions where change was needed; worked to clarify situations where information, instructions, or objectives are ambiguous; supported organizational change. Asked effective questions, sought additional information and used other appropriate techniques for clarifying the situation. Allowed limited time to acknowledge and engage their own feelings/stress, and then refocused on productivity. Willingly changed their work routine to incorporate the needed changes. Stayed objective, gathered helpful information, did nothing to upset the other person, and ideally tried to keep them calm as well. Helped the group prioritize change goals and provided practical guidance on how to implement. Spent minimal time engaging in negative thoughts, identified learning points, and moved on. Identified key learning points, and then refocused efforts toward high performance to the usual or a greater degree. Willingly aligned their work with the new priorities and abandoned past ways of doing things. Helped other(s) identify key aspects of the goal, and a series of concrete interim steps. Focused on facts and logic; monitored their thinking for interference from the stress.

Agility | Resilience

BEHAVIORAL QUESTIONS	RATING SCALE
9. Think of a potentially volatile or emotionally charged interaction where you needed to remain calm and professional. Walk me through how you handled the situation. 10. Tell me about a time when you helped a workgroup adapt to a change without disrupting productivity. 11. Describe a time when you interpreted a situation and information objectively despite being stressed and then took logical follow-up action. 12. For many people, implementing change is difficult. Walk me through how you helped someone translate a new change goal into practical implementation steps. 13. Often people are uncomfortable embracing an organizational change. Describe a time when you supported an organizational change effort — regardless of personal comfort in doing so. 14. Think about a setback or rejection you faced. Describe the steps you took to maintain high performance afterwards. 15. In this position, you will likely have some failures mixed in with your successes. Describe a time when you were highly effective at rebounding after a failure.	3: Attempted to clarify the situation that didn't result in a clear understanding of all the factors involved. Sloppy exit of previous project; stuff fell through the cracks. Excessive time spent finishing tasks whose priority had now become secondary. Resistance to or grudging acceptance of the organizational change. Restatement of obvious aspects that needed to change, but minimal practical guidance. Expected both adaptation and a high level of productivity without a clearly communicated process for accomplishing both. Decision-making and action were somewhat based in logic, but still heavily compromised by the effects of stress. 2: Unable to move quickly enough through change-"Analysis paralysis." Too much engagement in the emotional aspects of change and allowance of productivity to slip unnecessarily. Prolonged emotional response to the negative event, and too slow a return to high productivity. 1: Over-dependence on others to tell the candidate what to do. Hesitation, complaint or loss of productivity that may have undermined the desired change. Too long a period of frustration, disappointment, or apathy, interfering with productivity. 0: Unwilling to change

Agility | Resilience

BEHAVIORAL QUESTIONS	RATING SCALE
1. Tell me about a time when you were on a team and someone on the team wasn't pulling their weight. What did you do?	5: Approached the individual to find out the reason for the lack of participation. Addressed the cause in a non-threatening, non-demeaning way, improving the teammate's contributions, knowledge, skills, abilities, self-esteem and regard with the rest of the team. Earned trust and credibility by completing own share of the team's work; placed team priorities above own personal agenda; appropriately considered others' opinions on matters that affect the team; challenge proposed actions in a way that facilitated constructive discussion; supported team decisions, even if different from own opinion. Fulfilled their portion despite constraints, probably recognizing that this assignment presented an opportunity to truly earn trust. Sought out and worked effectively with others of diverse perspectives, talents, backgrounds, and/ or styles; contributed to a team climate in which differences were valued and supported; challenged any stereotyping or offensive comments; sought out and respond to feedback from others about their own behavior that might be perceived as biased. Productively applied each of their strengths or unique approaches. Stated recognition of ideas' positives and phrased challenges in a respectful and objective way. Asked people who were likely to have observed their behavior and who would respond truthfully, and then changed behavior as appropriate. Encouraged or reinforced action that was different from their own preferred approach. Knew or obtained relevant others' opinions and weighed them heavily in decision-making. Recognized occurrences of teamwork, ensured that information systems integrated with one another, ensured revision of incentive systems to promote it.
2. Describe a situation you've been involved in where you were required to work with other teams/departments. What was your role? How did you foster collaboration?	
3. Sometimes it's inevitable that two departments' priorities or expectations conflict. Tell me about a time when you were involved in this type of situation. How did you deal with it?	
4. Describe a situation in which you acted in support of someone else to assist them in addressing their issues and concerns.	
5. Can you give me an example of a time when you offered ideas and support to team members in ways that reduced conflict and increased cooperation?	
6. How have you sought and built relationships with other departments?	
7. Tell me about a challenging situation when you worked to earn trust and credibility within your team by completing your share of the team's work.	
8. Think of a work team you led that was made up of people with diverse perspectives or talents.	
9. Describe how you capitalized on these to accomplish a business objective.	

Collaboration | Teamwork

BEHAVIORAL QUESTIONS	RATING SCALE
10. How one challenges a proposed idea affects the quality of subsequent discussion. Describe a time when you challenged an idea in a way that promoted constructive discussion of alternative views. How did you do so? 11. Describe a situation in which you sought feedback about whether your behavior seemed biased against people of a certain work orientation or background. How did you respond to the feedback? 12. Describe a specific time when you contributed to a team climate where differences are valued and supported. 13. We believe that it is best to appropriately consider others' opinions on matters that affect them. Tell me about a time when you did this. 14. Describe an endeavor in which you ensured that organizational culture, systems, and processes enabled cross-functional teamwork. 15. Think of a time when you placed the priorities of your team above your own personal agenda. Walk me through how you did that. 16. Tell me about a situation when you provided full support for a team decision that you didn't agree with. 17. Describe a time when you sought out the diverse perspectives and talents of others to accomplish an objective.	Devoted substantial time and resources to the team priorities when they could have been investing it in their own. Cooperated fully, using normal diligence in acting on the decision, and/or praised the decision in discussions with non-team members. Purposely used the opinions or talents of people representing different backgrounds, approaches to work, or skills. 3: Performed adequately and in a non-noteworthy way. Provided small portions of time/resources, or invested as a result of a forced requirement. Relied on people who were simply available, rather than likely to bring different approaches. 2: Provided fair treatment and an equal distribution of work, but without consideration for others' unique approaches, or with different functional roles. Sought feedback either from people who wouldn't know or wouldn't be truthful, or made little effort to address biased behavior. Supported only a non-noteworthy difference. Little more than constant preaching about teamwork, but with little supportive action. 1: Evidence of objectivity and politeness, but with non-verbals indicative of sarcasm or condescension, thus sparking argument/defensiveness rather than constructive dialogue. Quickly dismissed others' opinions. Compromised action by the candidate to carry out the decision or public criticism of it. 0: Did nothing. Complained to the boss and to teammates.

Collaboration | Teamwork

BEHAVIORAL QUESTIONS	RATING SCALE
1. On your résumé, you pointed out this accomplishment of which you seemed really proud. How did you go about achieving it? 2. Think of a time when a project succeeded largely because you held a person or group accountable for achieving results. Tell me all about it. 3. Describe something you've done that illustrates your high personal work standards. 4. Describe a time when your sense of urgency about getting results contributed to a critical success.	5: Exceeded the goal successfully. Oriented to the bottom line. Steadfastly pushed self and others to obtain the goal. Demonstrated high personal work standards and a sense of urgency about results; did everything possible to meet goals and deadlines; persisted in the face of repeated challenges; accepted responsibility for the outcomes of their own work. Took action to ensure high customer satisfaction or quality, such as working overtime to meet a deadline, double-checking work, or revising something until customer was satisfied. Worked noteworthy extra hours, reprioritized other responsibilities, or secured additional resources. 3: Achieved success, but in a minimally challenging situation. 2: Achieved the goal, but without appropriate concern for effect on others, process, or ethics. Pressured others too strongly to achieve results, resulting in turnover. Focused on own achievement, rather than team achievement. Took unimpressive extra steps taken, such as a spot check. 1: Didn't deliver results consistently. Didn't get things done on time. Wasted time and resources pursuing non-essentials. Blamed others. Procrastinated. Did the least to get by. 0: No regard for results and goal achievement. Only focused on own personal agenda. Accepted excuses, inappropriate easing of standards, and/ or success due only to other factors.

Excellence

BEHAVIORAL QUESTIONS	RATING SCALE
1. Give me an example of how you have stayed up to date on trends in your field. 2. Share with me one particular example of a complex problem you solved using your knowledge and experience in your field. 3. Tell me about a time when a client used you to address an issue they were facing. What was your role? What specifically did you do to address the issue? What was the outcome? 4. Describe an example of when you played a key role in advancing your profession. Tell me about it.	5: 5+ years of experience + diverse application/success; Informed and knowledgeable in current practices and future trends affecting functional area; applied tactical and strategic mastery in area of expertise; viewed and leveraged as a subject matter expert by stakeholders 4: 3 – 5 years of experience + diverse application/success 3: 3 – 5 years of experience 2: 1 – 2 years of experience + diverse application/success 1: 1-2 years of experience 0: no experience

*Technical Skills ***

*Assumes that the area of expertise/technology has existed for this amount of time.

BEHAVIORAL QUESTIONS	RATING SCALE
1. When did you have to come up with a new way, approach, process, or solution to an existing or new challenge? What did you do and how did you implement it? 2. What new idea(s) have you championed that resulted in a new product/process or improvement? 3. Tell me about how you recently anticipated a problem before it occurred. 4. Conversely, tell me about how you failed to anticipate a problem before it occurred. What did you learn from the situation? 5. Give me an example of a time when you were not satisfied with the first answer and probed to identify underlying issues and helped to develop a creative solution. 6. On the other hand, give me an example of a time when you should have gone beyond the first answer but didn't and you failed to probe to identify underlying issues. 7. Describe a recent instance when you followed a systematic and consistent process when analyzing a complex problem. 8. How have you helped others think about issues to drive creative solutions? 9. Describe a success you've had resulting from applying a novel approach to a situation. 10. Describe a time when you have independently applied your professional expertise in unique or innovative ways.	5: Came up with many new and unique ideas. Easily made connections among previously unrelated notions. Generated creative ideas to solve problems and improve work methods; applied novel approaches to situations; independently applied professional expertise in unique/innovative ways; collaborated with team members to brainstorm creative approaches; rethought situations to create new opportunities or overcome obstacles. Generated "out-of-the-box" ideas employing approaches that were uncommon to their environment. Made a practical improvement that was successfully implemented due to a careful adaptation of a technical skill or application of expertise to a new area. Applied idea to a real opportunity in a practical way, resulting in a useful application. Facilitated an approach not common to the group or organizational culture, and achieved positive impact/success. Revisited a paradigm, value, or assumption, and acted in a way that was divergent, yet effective, with the old approach. Suggested ideas, parted with them appropriately upon others' review, and build on the ideas of others. Suggested a novel approach, or a new application of a familiar approach, that could easily be implemented. 3: Employed only trivial variation to old approaches, or a novel approach that resulted in a minimal impact. Made only a minor or unimpressive adjustment to an established solution. Made an obvious change based only on new information, or passive compliance with others' innovative efforts. Considered only obvious/conventional alternatives or unique but unrealistic ones.

Creativity | Innovation

BEHAVIORAL QUESTIONS	RATING SCALE
11. Describe a time when you were able to build on someone else's suggestion or idea, and it turned into a new approach or an improvement to a previous approach.	2: Was over-infatuated with marginally productive new ideas and wasted time. Got involved in too many new things at once, without focus. Did not follow through on the idea or on the details. Wasted time in pursing an idea that had no value to the business at hand.
12. Tell me about an experience when you applied an innovative solution to improve the group's performance.	
13. Think of a time when you overcame an obstacle or created a new opportunity by rethinking a situation. Walk me through how you approached it.	1: Relied on existing processes and procedures, disregarding/ discounting novel approaches/options. Narrow, tactical, cautious, and conservative in approach. Didn't connect ideas outside own area. Ineffective force-fit of technical skills or reverting to familiar ways of doing things.
14. Tell me about a success you had in collaborating with team members to brainstorm creative approaches.	0: Did nothing.
15. Tell me about a time when you generated a creative idea to solve a problem or improve a work method.	

Creativity | Innovation

BEHAVIORAL QUESTIONS	RATING SCALE
10. Describe a challenging situation that demonstrates your skill in dealing effectively with people to accomplish your work.	to communicate actively within or outside these meetings, and facilitated an environment where tactful, open communication was accepted and taken seriously. Repeated back key aspects of what was said, asked about logical inferences, and/or took similar steps. Expressed appreciation for the other person's opinion, tried to understand it and act on it. Made a persuasive and impactful case for the value of diverse perspectives in improving decision-making. Used different channels (email, presentations, 1:1 meetings, etc.) to accomplish different goals. Maintained contact with people who had useful knowledge, resources, or skills, and leveraged such people to accomplish their work or goal.
11. Think of a time when you worked closely with someone who clearly had a different perspective, background, or style from yours.	
12. How did you work effectively with this person despite your differences?	
13. Active and constructive dialogue is critical to healthy growth and maintenance of an organization. Describe a time when you created venues to facilitate this.	
14. Describe a time when you used active and attentive listening skills to verify that you understood correctly.	3: Advised others to communicate, but without constructive guidance about doing so effectively. Little more than repetition of the vision/mission/objectives in abstract terms. Provided obviously needed information, showing no truly proactive focus by the candidate, or forwarded vast amounts of information without making the relevance clear. Held meetings too infrequently or too small in scope. Proactively and persistently sought out people who might lead to the target individual.
15. Tell me about a situation where you responded constructively to a difference of opinion. What did you do and say?	
16. Describe a time when you networked your way to an influential person.	
17. Think of a time when you encouraged others to stay open to, seek, and learn from diverse perspectives and feedback. What did you do?	
18. Describe a situation that required you to use multiple communication channels to reach various audiences with a strategic message. What channels did you use and why?	2: Showed a token effort to make contacts, coincidental contact, and/or minimal follow-up with contacts around the organization. Was only self-aware of their most extreme behaviors. Negligible differences and basic adherence to their own preferred style. Nothing more than delivery of the same message the same way to multiple audiences, with specific data being replaced as appropriate. Was courteous, but with little other indication of effective work interaction.
19. Having a network of technical and business contacts can help in a variety of ways. Describe a time when you used such a network to help you meet the responsibilities of your job.	

Respect

BEHAVIORAL QUESTIONS	RATING SCALE
Respect	Accepted unclear information, resulting in misunderstanding. Little effort to understand, perhaps with a brief, polite but unappreciative statement of thanks. Little more than a brief admonishment to someone to not be closed-minded. Over-relied on certain channels, resulting in inefficiency or low impact. Relied on people who were easily accessible, but who lacked critical skills / knowledge / contacts. 1: Created disagreement for its own sake, a counterproductive presentation, or a thoughtless retraction upon challenge. Excessively procrastinated, or made a point wrongly / prematurely in the heat of the moment. Compromised business interaction because of disrespect for the other person's approach or background. Fostered an environment that punished, ignored, or otherwise didn't reinforce open communication. Relied on a limited number of contacts who repeatedly proved to be ineffective.

Questionable Questions:

	PERMISSIBLE	ILLEGAL / ACTIONABLE
Address / Residence	"Can you be reached at this address? If not, would you care to provide us with another?" "Can you be reached at these telephone numbers? If not, would you care to provide us with another?"	"Do you own your home or rent?" "Do you live with your spouse?" "With whom do you live?" "What part of town do you live in?"
Age	Only ask questions that verify non-minor status, such as: "Are you over 18?" "If hired, can you show proof of age?" "If under 18, can you, after employment, submit a work permit?"	"How old are you?" "What is your date of birth?" "What is your age?" "When were you born?" "When/what dates did you attend elementary or high school?" Avoid questions, comments, or words with any implication of preference for workers under 40 years of age.
AIDS/HIV or Disability	"Are you able to perform the essential functions of this job either with or without a reasonable accommodation?" (Seek only a Yes or No answer, no explanation). "Are you currently able to perform the essential duties of the job(s) for which you are applying?" If the disability is obvious or disclosed, you may ask about accommodations.	"Are you disabled?" "Have you ever filed for or received workers' compensation?" "What medical problems/conditions do you have?" "How much sick time or medical leave did you take at your last employer?" "How and when did you become disabled?" "What types of disabilities does your family have?"
Arrests / Convictions	"Have you ever been convicted of a criminal offense (excluding convictions that were sealed, eradicated, or expunged, or that may have resulted in a referral to a diversion program)?" "Are there any criminal charges currently pending against you?"	"Have you ever been in trouble with the law? What kind?" "Have you ever been arrested?" Any question regarding an arrest that did not result in a conviction. Any question regarding criminal records that have been sealed, eradicated, or expunged.
Citizenship / Birthplace	ASKED OF ALL APPLICANTS: "Are you authorized to work in the U.S.? If hired, you will be required to submit verification of your legal right to work in the United States?"	"Are you a United States citizen?" "Where were you born?" "What is your citizenship?" "From where is your accent?" "Are your parents/spouse native-born or naturalized?" "What are your naturalization plans?" Any questions regarding birthplace or citizenship status of applicant, applicant's spouse, parents, or other relatives.

	PERMISSIBLE	ILLEGAL / ACTIONABLE
Color / Race	State that a photograph may be required after employment.	Any questions concerning race or color of skin, eyes, hair, etc.
Court Records	"Has a court, jury, or government agency ever made a finding that you committed unlawful harassment or discrimination?"	"Have you ever had a bankruptcy?" "Have you ever sued or filed claims or complaints against your employer?" "Have you ever been a plaintiff in a lawsuit?"
Drug Use	"Do you currently use any illegal drugs?" "Have you recently used any illegal drugs?"	Questions about past addictions. Questions about use of prescription drugs. Questions about frequency of alcohol use.
Emergency Contact	"What are the name, telephone number, and address of the person to be notified in case of an accident or emergency?"	"What are the name, telephone number, and address of the relative to be notified in case of accident or emergency?"
Experience / Skills / Activities	"Do you have any special work-related skills or knowledge?" "Are your skills recent?" "How will your involvement in [activity] affect your work here?"	"Does your physical condition make you less skilled?"

	PERMISSIBLE	ILLEGAL / ACTIONABLE
Economic Status	"This position requires working on-site [state the job's standard schedule]. Are you able to work the required schedule?"	"Do you have any past or current bankruptcies?" "Do you play golf?" "How did you get to the interview today?" "How were you affected by the recent downturn in stock investments?" "What is your credit rating?" "What kind of car do you drive?" "What school do your children attend?" "Where did you go on your last vacation?" "Where exactly do you live?"
Education	"Are you currently enrolled or do you intend to enroll in school?" "In which subjects did you excel in school?" "What did you select as your major?" "Are you interested in continuing your education? Why? When? Where?" "Did you education prepare you for the job you are seeking with us? In what ways?"	"Who paid for your educational expenses while you were in school?" "Did you go to school on a scholarship?" "Do you still owe on student loans taken out during school?" "When did you graduate from high school/college?"
Family	"Do you have any commitments that would prevent you from working regular hours?" "Can you work overtime, if needed?" "Are you now or do you expect to be engaged in any other business or employment? If so, what kind of business or employment is it? How much time does it require?"	"How many children do you have?" "Do you have children? How old are they?" "Tell me about how you manage your work/life balance." "Who takes care of your children while you are working?" "What kind of childcare arrangements do you have?" "Do your children go to day care?" "What does your husband/wife/spouse/partner think about your working outside the home?" "What does your husband/wife/spouse/partner do?" "What is your husband/wife/spouse/partner's salary?" "What is your husband/wife/spouse/partner's name? What are your children's names?"

	PERMISSIBLE	ILLEGAL / ACTIONABLE
Marital Status	"Please state the name(s) of any relatives already employed by us or one of our competitors." "Whom should we contact in case of an emergency?"	"Is it Mrs. or Miss?" "Are you single? Married? Divorced? Separated? Engaged? Widowed?" "Do you have a domestic partner?" "What is your maiden name?" "Who is your spouse/partner?"
Military Service	"Have you served in the U.S. military?" "Did your military service and training provide you with skills you could put to use in this job?"	"Have you served in the army of a foreign country?" "What type of discharge did you receive from the U.S. military service?" "Can you provide discharge papers?"
Name	"Have you ever used another name?" "Is any additional information related to change of name, use of an assumed name, or nickname necessary to enable a check on your work and educational record?"	"What is your maiden name?"
National Origin	"Are you prevented from being employed in the United States because of visa or immigration status?"	"What is your national origin?" "Where were you born?" "What is the origin of your name?" "What is your native language?" "What country do your ancestors come from?" "Do you read, write, or speak another foreign language (not required in the job)?" "How did you learn to speak this foreign language?" Any questions pertaining to the nationality, lineage, ancestry, national origin, descent, or parentage of applicant, applicant's parents, or spouse/partner.

	PERMISSIBLE	ILLEGAL / ACTIONABLE
Organizations	"To which professional associations do you belong?" "Of which professional and job-related organizations/ associations are you an active member? "What positions have you held in these organizations?"	Questions about all the organizations, clubs, societies, and lodges to which the candidate belongs.
Pregnancy	"How long do you plan to stay on the job?" "Are you currently able to perform the essential duties of the job(s) for which you are applying?"	"Are you pregnant?" "When was your most recent pregnancy terminated?" "Do you plan on becoming pregnant?" Any questions about medical history concerning pregnancy and pregnancy-related matters.
Past Employment	"How did you overcome challenges you faced there?" "Which problems frustrated you the most?" "Of the jobs you've held, which did you enjoy the most and why?" "What were your reasons for leaving your previous jobs?" "Have you ever been discharged from any position? If so, for what reason(s)?" "Can you meet the attendance requirements of this job?"	"How many sick days did you take at your old job?" "Did you file any claims against your former employer?" "Have you sustained any work-related injury?"
Religion or Creed	"This position requires working on-site [state the job's standard schedule]. Are you able to work the required schedule?" "Are you available to work on nights and weekends?" (if there is a legitimate business reason)	"What is your religion?" "What church do you go to?" "What are your religious holidays?" "Does your religion prevent you from working night, weekends, or holidays?"
Sexual Orien-tation		"Are you gay/lesbian/bisexual/ transgendered?" "Do you have a domestic partner?" "What is your view on same-sex partner benefits?"

SELF: What is your understanding of the expectations around your role in Recruiting and Hiring? What are your expectations of the stakeholders in the process (recruiters, interviewers, candidates, etc.)? How can and will you make them better aware of your explicit expectations? How can and will you optimize the candidate experience (and showcase your organization in the best light) by being more explicit about your expectations in the process and managing the candidate's expectations?

TEAM: What are your team members' expectations and needs from you around Recruiting and Hiring? Do they expect to interview potential candidates who will become colleagues and have input into their selection? What is your gameplan to ensure that you become aware of their expectations, make them more explicit, and that your team is aware of your process?

ORGANIZATION: What are your organization's expectations about your role in Recruiting and Hiring? Some organizations expect managers to be constantly recruiting for their organization (presence on LinkedIn, at professional associations, conferences, etc.) – is this an expectation of you? Who does your organization identify and reward for making excellent hires? What is it they do? How can you gain more insight into their work and explore their support/mentoring of you in this area? How can these be made more explicit? What can and will you do to make improvements in this area?

REALITY CHECK: What are the metrics around your organization's average time-to-hire? What is your organization's regrettable turnover rate (people who the organization didn't want to voluntarily leave)? How does your organization fare as a "great place to work" when compared to your competitors (benefits, time off, work environment, strategy, profitability, career development options, etc.)? What does your organization offer that your competitors can't (what's your organization's not easily replicable niche)? How does your organization treat/notify candidates who are not selected for hire? How are applicants who aren't being considered notified? What does the communication sounds like? Does it make the applicant/candidate likely to reapply to your organization doesn't want to have leave voluntarily)? How can you use this data to help make you an even more effective hiring manager and create positive changes in your organization's hiring and recruitment processes? How can these be more explicit? What can and will you do to positively impact this area?

CHAPTER 4

CREATING EFFECTIVE ON-BOARDING PLANS

Once a candidate has accepted an offer to come to work at your organization, your role as the manager becomes even more important in the employee's experience. Remember that employees leave managers, not organizations.

Tools to use in this part of the employee's lifecycle include:

- Manager Checklist for New Hire Start
- The 30-60-90 Day Plan
- Check-Ins and One-on-Ones

As soon as a start date has been negotiated/decided, please ensure that your new hire will be able to feel welcomed and well-resourced on arrival:

- Make sure you are in the office/available on the employee's first day and set up the expectation of open dialogue (including scheduling regular one-on-ones)
- E-mail address/access
- Relevant systems access
- Cell phone
- Laptop
- Workstation/office (if on-site)
- Communication to the team about the new hire, including setting up time to meet them
- Match your new hire with an experienced, role model member of the team *who welcomes and is even more engaged*

by this additional responsibility and has the capacity to take this on
(rotate this assignment to other exemplar team members
for future new hires so that the same team members isn't
always expected to perform this task on top of their existing workload)

- A welcome "gift" – lunch with you/the team? Gift card?
Company swag? (sent to home, if remote)

Meet with your new hire to explicitly state expectations for the first
90 days and set goals, KPIs, and priorities. Continue to meet with
your new hire weekly until a different cadence is needed/mutual-
ly-decided upon. Have them create and complete a 90-Day Plan into
which you provide input, support in the appropriate areas (identify-
ing the key stakeholders with which to be met, validating the plan),
and check on progress.

	DURING FIRST 30 DAYS	30 – 60 DAYS	60 – 90 DAYS & ON-GOING
Role Goals	*Understand the organization, your role and how you fit in. Make contacts that provide a broad overview of functions, culture, people, successes and challenges.*	*Develop a Strategy/Plan for initial success utilizing the experience and advice from your manager and insight from your new network.*	*Implement & execute. Stay aware of business challenges, resources and your own strengths and areas for development.*
Company	Complete all required/ mandatory company training, including New Hire Orientation and compliance trainings.		
Your Department	Meet with all team members / key stakeholders to start forming productive and effective relationships and gain an understanding of the company, while building your inside and outside teams. Ask: What are the biggest challenges the organization is facing or will face in the future? Why is the organization facing such challenges? What are the most promising opportunities for the organization? What needs to happen for the organization to realize those opportunities? If you were me, where would you focus attention? Complete all systems training	With your manager, co-create your annual goals.	**5 Pillars of Self-Efficacy** Adopt success strategies Set priorities Have a monthly "touch base" with your boss Enforce personal disciplines Build and meet with your support network as needed

	DURING FIRST 30 DAYS	30 – 60 DAYS	60 – 90 DAYS & ON-GOING
You	Organize workspace for maximum efficiency and productivity. Gather information and "evidence" to get a clearer understanding of the company culture, your group's culture, and your department/team culture so that you can operate successfully within those norms and parameters. Sign up for benefits, direct deposit, etc. Schedule (bi-)weekly 1:1s with your manager.	Check out and become involved with the organization's Employee Resource Groups and/or Community Outreach Activities. Sign up for any relevant training classes that address your development objectives.	What are your strengths and how can you leverage them? What are your vulnerabilities in your new job? How do you plan to compensate for them? What personal disciplines do you need to develop/enhance most? How can you gain more control over your local environment? What support relationships do you have and which are your highest priorities? What are your priorities for strengthening your advice and support network, internally and externally? In what areas do you need support (technically, politically, personally)?

For a deeper dive on this, check out the source work of Michael Watkins (see the *Sources & Additional Resources* section).

During the on-boarding of team members (or if clarity around roles/responsibilities and accountabilities is needed later on), consider using a RACI Matrix. This is a framework designed to help the user identify and make explicit roles and responsibilities associated with a specific project, business process, or deliverable. It is also referred to as a Responsibility Assignment Matrix or Linear Responsibility Chart.

TASK | ACTIVITY | PROJECT STEP	DUE BY	NAME 1	NAME 2	NAME 3	NAME 4	NAME 5	NAME 6	NAME 7	NAME 8	NAME 9	NAME 10	NAME 11	NAME 12	IMPLICATION OF FAILURE	STATUS UPDATE
1.															
2.															
3.															
4.															
5.															
6.															
7.															
8.															
9.															
10.															
11.															
12.															

PROJECT/PROCESS NAME — Decision

How to Use It:

User identifies team members and stakeholders associated with a specific project and populates their names in the appropriate parts of the matrix so that there is certainty and clarity about who is responsible for each part of a project or deliverable. The matrix is then shared with the stakeholders so that they all know their individual roles and expectations of them on the task. Role assignments include who is directly Responsible for tasks/activities getting done in a high quality way (per the Approver's direction), whose Approval is needed before action is taken (the ultimate owner of the process/project and no further escalation is needed), whose Consultation is needed for input and consent prior to decisions and actions, and those who simply need to be Informed of what has been decided (and may provide additional information or opinions while not being directly involved in the decision-making). Other key roles that may be called out include Support (resources allocated to the Responsible party who assist in completing the task) and even those strategically and purposely Out of the Loop/Omitted).

Success Factors:

- Inclusion of all necessary parties in the appropriate spot on the matrix
- Constant flow of communication to the stakeholders

For a deeper dive on this, check out the Project Management Institute's PMBOK Guide (see *Sources & Additional Resources* section).

SELF: Think back to your on-boarding. What worked well for you? What were your expectations of how it would be? What do you wish could have been different/better? How could you have been more explicit in expectations? What can and will you do to make this process better, more effective, and more welcoming, resulting in faster employee readiness, assimilation/integration, and productivity?

TEAM: When a new team member starts, what are their expectations of what will happen to help support their success? How are existing team members included in the process? What are their expectations around this? How are existing team members notified of a new team member's hire, start, role, new interdependencies, etc.? How can and will these be made more explicit?

ORGANIZATION: What are your organization's expectations of your role in on-boarding your team? What support is provided to you to make this happen? How can and will these be made more explicit?

REALITY CHECK: What actually happens when a new hire joins your organization? Is the on-boarding experience consistent? Are they able to be "up-and-running" on their first day? Do they have all the equipment and access to the systems they'll need to do their jobs? What can you do to eliminate some of these stressors and facilitate their successful on-boarding experience? What can and will you do to make your expectations of organizational support more explicit?

CHAPTER 5

GOAL-SETTING

Some truths about Goals and Goal-Setting:

- We need goals so that we have directionality in performance and so that we can measure our progress in meeting the needs and expectations of our customers, stakeholders, and leaders, in ultimate achievement of our mission and vision.
- We can't hold people accountable to goals that are not explicitly stated and understood/agreed-to.
- Goals are most powerful and best understood/committed to when they are co-created and not simply handed down as a mandate.
- Goals are NOT static. They can – and will – change as a result of competitive business and volatile social conditions. The new goals must be made just as explicit and understood as the original goals, and must replace, not be added to the original expectations.
- Goal-Setting, Tracking, and Feedback/Coaching are MANAGEMENT NON-NEGOTIABLE EXPECTATIONS/SUCCESS FACTORS
  1. **Set clear, specific, and measurable expectations around performance and behavior**
     - ○ Goals/Results – what we expect people to achieve (tangible/objective)
     - ○ Traits/Competencies/Behaviors (intangible/subjective) – how we expect people to act/behave

- o Skills - The specific things that people must possess in order to accomplish the tasks to achieve the results
- o Norms - A code of conduct or behavioral agreement for how we are going to act and behave with each other
- o Ensure/Validate that team members have the skill, will, and understanding of what's expected of them

2. **Monitor & track performance and behavior**
   - o Goals/Results – what we expect people to achieve tracked through organizational metrics, balanced scorecards and dashboards (objective/tangible)
   - o Balanced scorecard - The way in which to measure, monitor, track, and improve business based upon a set of outcomes
   - o Behaviors – through observation, 360-degree feedback, 'management by walking around,' 'catching people doing things right'

3. **Provide frequent feedback on performance and behavior** *(See section on Feedback)*
   - o Positive and developmental
   - o One-on-ones
   - o Hallway coaching moments
   - o Structured coaching opportunities
   - o Our System

To ensure expectations around goals are explicit and understood, goals should follow the "SMARTEST" formula:

- Specific – clear, concise, well-defined, explicit, shared with others for accountability
- Measurable – progress and achievement can be measured by a specific deadline/within a specific timeframe by which the goal is expected to be achieved (if no new other goal takes precedence)
- Attainable – achievable, yet appropriately and realistically aggressive/aspirational
- Relevant – important and aligned with organization's values and goals, and under the auspices of the role and the skills of the employee
- Time-bound – within the evaluation period (Hourly? Daily? Weekly? Monthly? Quarterly? Annually?)
- Evaluated & Revisable as necessary, based on changing business conditions, needs, and new direction
- Satisfying – meaningful, satisfying, engaging, and energizing to the employee
- Team-Based – how is the team (*all* members of the team) being recognized for its achievement of goals requiring interdependency of team members? Who decides?

Cascade them!

- Leaders set goals first and share them with their teams
- Each team member identifies which of their leader's goals their role supports and creates their version relevant to the achievement of that goal, based on their scope of authority (their role may not necessarily align with each one of them, and that's OK)

ACTION VERB	WHAT WILL CHANGE	SUCCESS MEASURE(S)	DUE DATE
• Increase • Decrease • Maintain • Improve • Reduce • Maximize • Minimize • Achieve • Attain • Sustain • Maintain • Lessen • Lower • Raise	• Productivity • Sales • Satisfaction • Morale • Savings • Quality • Profitability • Loss	• By x% • By $x • By x points	• By _____

KEY PERFORMANCE INDICATORS

You will inevitably hear the acronym "KPIs" – which stands for "Key Performance Indicators" – used interchangeably with "Goals." Keep in mind that if your goals are too broad or general, thinking of and defining them in terms of KPIs can be a good reminder of how to ensure that you are tracking on achieving your and your team's overall objectives.

Here are some tips for choosing and using KPIs:

- Start with your goals. What do you want to achieve? Once you know your goals, you can start to identify the KPIs that will help you track your progress.
- Make sure your KPIs are measurable. You need to be able to quantify your KPIs so that you can track your progress over time.
- Set targets for your KPIs. This will provide a benchmark against which to measure progress.
- Track KPIs regularly. This will help to identify areas for focus and improvement.

- Use KPIs in decision-making. The insights gained from KPIs should be used to make informed decisions about how to improve the organization.

SELF: What are the expectations of your role in goal-setting for your own goals? For your team members' goals? Do you create them for yourself and share with your boss? Do you co-create them with your boss? Are they changeable? If so, how do you know if/when they've changed? How can and will you make this more explicitly communicated and understood by all parties involved?

TEAM: What are your team members' expectations about your and their roles in goal-setting? What happens when business needs, direction, and goals change? How is this communicated? How are goals updated to reflect this? How can and will you make this more explicitly understood?

ORGANIZATION: What are your organization's expectations around goal-setting and achievement? How is this rewarded? What support is provided to you to make this happen? How can and will you make this easier, more relevant, more effective, and overall better?

REALITY CHECK: How often are goals revisited and updated in a formal way, ensuring expectations are explicit and valid? How is goal achievement tied to performance reviews, ratings, and rewards (compensation increases, bonuses, etc.)? How can and will you influence this so that expectations around the goal-setting process and the relationship to performance management are more explicitly understood and practiced?

CHAPTER 6

CHECK-INS & ONE-ON-ONES

Consistent and regular two-way communication with our employees is critical to ensuring:

- Alignment with and clarity around current strategy and direction
- Accountability around progress being made toward agreed-upon goal completion
- Roadblocks, hurdles, and challenges are identified and resolved as early on as possible
- Team members are engaged in the work they are doing
- Workload allocation is appropriate and equitable
- Trust is being built between team members and their managers

As such, frequent, scheduled, and conducted check-ins are an *Explicit Expectation* of all managers.

- Check-ins are frequent (ideally, weekly), informal, employee-centered conversations between employees and their managers
- Check-ins are a time for the team member to ask for what they need from their manager to help them meet their goals, where coaching and co-solutioning may take place. Focus on:
    o Team member's career and aspirations
    o Connections that need to be made within your organization to help them be more effective in current and future/aspirational roles

- ○ Team member's capabilities and capacity (needs for training, development, workload rebalance)
  - ○ Team member's contributions (expectations, alignment to goals, recognition)
- Ideally, an employee is empowered to schedule the check-ins on a cadence that works for them (since this is their meeting).
- Feel free to use these check-in conversation starters:
  - "What do you want to focus on today?"
  - "What challenges or concerns do you have?"
  - "What's working? What's not? What alternatives do you have?"
  - "How can I help? Would you like me to …?"

NOTE: Check-ins should NOT be used for:

- assigning additional work, projects
- conducting a performance review conversation
- conducting a compensation discussion

Separately-scheduled one-on-one meetings (one-on-ones) should be used for these purposes, to preserve the purpose, intent, and integrity of the check-in meetings.

Many organizations struggle with accountability and holding each other accountable. Consider asking these questions during your 1:1s to support and drive explicit expectations around focus and results:

- "What is your understanding of our team's/department's current priorities and what is expected of you in your role to achieve them?"
- "What are you currently working on to support these?"
- "What are you currently working on that does not support these?"
- "What will you stop doing to refocus on this quarter's priorities?"

- "What will you start/continue doing to refocus on this quarter's priorities?"
- "What support do you need to make this happen?"
- "What barriers or challenges do you anticipate in stopping lower priority work (from stakeholders, partners, peers, internal/external customers, manager/leadership, etc.)?"
- "What additional feedback, coaching, incentive/disincentive would be helpful for you to refocus your time/energy?"
- "How can we make sure that we hold each other accountable to these commitments? What happens if/when we don't?"

All check-ins are one-on-ones, but not all one-on-ones are check-ins.

 SELF: What are YOUR expectations around your role in conducting check-ins and one-on-ones? What are your expectations about engaging in check-ins and one-on-ones with YOUR boss? How explicitly communicated and understood are these? How can and will you make this a regular, productive practice that doesn't get deprioritized? How can and will you explicitly separate check-ins from goal- and performance-related one-on-ones so that the intent and expectations of each are fully understood by each party?

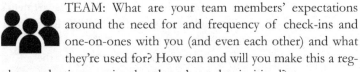 TEAM: What are your team members' expectations around the need for and frequency of check-ins and one-on-ones with you (and even each other) and what they're used for? How can and will you make this a regular, productive practice that doesn't get deprioritized?

ORGANIZATION: What are your organization's explicit expectations around check-ins and one-on-ones?

 REALITY CHECK: What are check-ins and one-on-ones *really* used for in your organization? How looked-forward-to are they? Or dreaded? How often are they held/canceled/rescheduled? How does your organization support/encourage having 1:1s? Is it in your goals? Are there support resources, training, and materials? How can and will you positively influence this?

CHAPTER 7

PRIORITIZATION, DELEGATION, & EMPOWERMENT

After goals have been set for your department/function/organization, it may become necessary to alter them as changes in the environment or strategy require us to pivot to new priorities. As new priorities are identified and cascaded, reprioritization of existing work needs to take place to ensure that our resources and energies are being focused on the right activities and outputs. The Urgent/Important Matrix is a great tool to use to categorize annual goals for the department/function/organization overall, then have each individual interpret those into their own Matrix, to be revisited monthly, or as new goals and priorities are determined.

Based on Stephen Covey's popularization of former U.S. President Dwight D. Eisenhower's practice, the Urgent/Important Matrix is a framework to help people categorize and prioritize the tasks and activities they do so that they focus their time on the ones most important to achieving their long-term goals. It may help to operationally define (and even relabel) "Urgent" as anything that has an immediate deadline for completion: "Time-Sensitive." "Important" can be thought of and relabeled as "Goal-Relevant" (where the goals are the goals to which you are being held accountable for accomplishment).

Summary of Use:

1. List all the activities and projects you feel you have to do, including everything that takes up your time at work, however unimportant it may seem/be

2. Plot them into each of the 4 quadrants of the Urgent/
   Important Matrix according to the following rubric:
   - Understanding the difference between "Important/
     Goal-Relevant" and "Urgent/Time-Sensitive" tasks
     and consciously and conscientiously focusing on com-
     pleting and achieving the important ones: Important/
     Goal-Relevant activities have an outcome that leads
     to the achievement of your goals whereas Urgent/
     Time-Sensitive activities demand immediate attention
     and have immediate consequences, and are often asso-
     ciated with the achievement of other peoples' goals.
   - Ensure that all stakeholders and anyone who has
     expectations based on prior prioritization are aware
     and in support of any new reprioritization and will
     have your back when previously Important/Goal-
     Relevant activities become deprioritized in favor
     of another, more immediate need. It CANNOT be
     something that is added IN ADDITION to your cur-
     rent scope for prioritization and expectations, as that
     will lead to burnout, frustration, disengagement, and
     lack of trust in leadership.
   - Engage in appropriate delegation of the "Urgent/
     Time-Sensitive" and Not Important/Not Goal-
     Relevant activities quadrant via the best practices
     below.
   - Have each team member create their own "Urgent/
     Important" Matrix, based on the goals expected of
     them to achieve. This is a directional and living doc-
     ument; revisit it and review it often with each team
     member to ensure appropriate focus of attention,
     expectation setting, performance, and bandwidth.

For a deeper dive, check out Stephen Covey's source
work (see the *Sources & Additional Resources* section).

	URGENT / TIME-SENSITIVE	NOT (AS) URGENT / TIME-SENSITIVE
IMPORTANT/GOAL-RELEVANT	**DO IT!** *In service of the vision/mission/ values/goals/operating principles*	**SCHEDULE IT!** *In service of the vision/mission/ values/goals/operating principles*
NOT (AS) IMPORTANT/GOAL-RELEVANT	**DELEGATE/PUSH BACK!** *What can I delegate to someone else, maybe even to our broader network (internally or externally)?*	**DON'T DO IT!** *What can I stop doing because it doesn't make sense or add value (any more)?*

<u>**Important/Goal-Relevant**</u> activities have an outcome that leads to the achievement of your goals.

<u>**Urgent/Time-Sensitive**</u> activities demand immediate attention and have immediate consequences, and are often associated with the achievement of other peoples' goals.

DELEGATION BEST PRACTICES

Only do the things that only you can do and that are relevant to the achievement of your goals. Delegate the rest with clear and explicit expectations.

- Make an inventory of everything you do during a typical week.
- Plot everything into your own Urgent/Important Matrix.
- Critically review the list and decide what can be done only by you (that supports your passions and unique capabilities).
- See what others can pick up (invite their aspirations and interests).
- Set clear and explicit expectations, perhaps using the "reasonable plus" (reasonable to a client's expectations and an organization would reasonably offer, plus a little extra) approach. Ask delegates to write down what they think they need to do and send it back to you for review/vetting before they get started.
- Communicate in **intent statements** – a concise summary of guidance that empowers employees rather than giving them so much detail that it spoils their creativity or stunts their initiative.
- Purpose: the "why." Why are we doing this project, plan, initiative, or reorganization?
- Method: Specify any non-negotiable, required tasks. Include only the most important tasks. Do not overdo this step (as it might lead to micromanaging).
- Risk: Specify how much risk you are willing to underwrite without your express permission (Capital risk? Risk of loss of a client?). Include any outcomes or actions that you do NOT want to happen.
- End State: Answer the questions, "If we are successful in achieving our intent, what will the outcome look like? What will success look like?"

- Review the list every few weeks and confirm that you are sticking to what you decided is only yours to do.
- Ask a trusted colleague/advisor/mentor to provide you with direct feedback if they notice you are slipping back into your old ways.
- Stay focused on your vision and mission.

Ultimately, delegation done right leads to empowerment of the organization's team members, increasing engagement and developing/preparing your team members for their next roles. To help managers and employees have additional clarity and set explicit expectations around empowerment, consider providing your team members with and adhering to these guidelines and guardrails:

1. (How and why) is this the right thing to do (for me, the team, the company)?
2. (How) will it positively impact other areas? What are the potential repercussions on others (colleagues/stakeholders/customers)?
3. (How) does it support my/our goals? (How/why) is it the most efficient option? How will it affect cost/budget? (How) does it support or promote our brand/image in a positive way?
4. (How) does this present an opportunity to pursue patent protection? (How) does this solution bring a unique value that is not easily replicable by others/our competitors? (How) is it elegant?
5. Is there data/research/evidence to support that this is the logical action to take?
6. What are our back-up plans if this fails? What are the consequences if this desired outcome isn't achieved or if we don't take any action?
7. (How) does this allow for growth now and in the future? What are my other options? What are the likely positive outcomes?
8. Is this within my scope of authority/purview to control and execute?

9. (How) does this fit within and affect the overall system? (How) is it sustainable?

You may decide to coach them to consider all nine perspectives, a select few that make more sense to your organization and align to its core values, or a subset of their own choosing. The important part is that, if they have shown a good faith effort to seriously and broadly consider their proposed solution from a variety of angles and risks with positive, critical, and objective intent, that you will support them and have their back, regardless of the positive or negative outcomes, results, and consequences. Recognize, celebrate, and reward the successes as well as the learnings (for future application) from all well-intentioned and well-thought-out efforts.

> For a deeper dive on this, check out my other business book, *The How and Why: Taking Care of Business with the Enneagram* (see the *Sources & Additional Resources* section).

 SELF: How comfortable are you at letting go and delegating tasks? What do you fear happening if you do so? What are your expectations around delegation? How will you make them explicit? How can and will you ensure you don't cross the line into micromanagement?

TEAM: What are your team members' expectations when something is delegated to them? What do they expect from you throughout the project? How do you know? How do they know? What can and will you do to ensure that their expectations are explicit and known by you, and that your expectations are explicit and known by them, so that you can best support their success?

ORGANIZATION: What are your organization's explicit expectations around what gets done by you and what gets done by your team members? Who is held accountable? How? Who in your organization is regarded and rewarded for their skills in time management, prioritization, productivity, goal achievement, and delegation? What is it they do? How can and will you gain more insight into their work and explore their support/mentoring of you in this area?

 REALITY CHECK: How many goals are you being held accountable for by your boss? When a new project or demand becomes a priority, what else is deprioritized or removed? How common are these conversations in your organization? What can you do to influence making this a standard practice, where there are explicit expectations set around what really is currently important to be working on, and that workloads are sustainable and realistic?

CHAPTER 8

COACHING & OTHER LEADERSHIP STYLES

Some truths and assumptions about coaching and development:

- All managers are expected to use coaching as part of their repertoire in leading, guiding, motivating, and developing their teams.
- People are capable of growth and development, if they choose to do so. People are naturally creative, resourceful, and whole.
- When coaching, we focus on and engage the whole person.
- Coaching is an effective way of developing others as it is a way in which managers ask questions to prompt and guide their employees to solve problems on their own. In this way, team members become more committed to the decision or solution, more so than having been told the answer or what to do. This also makes them more likely to come up with solutions to future challenges on their own rather than possibly becoming (co)dependent on their managers.
- Coaching is best used with employees who are in the second phase of the employee lifecycle (based on the Situational Leadership model).
- Organizations hire fully-capable and whole human beings who are able to solve problems on their own, sometimes needing coaching from their colleagues or managers.

What exactly is Coaching?

- Coaching is a leadership style, providing a way to effectively empower people, encouraging and supporting them on their path to *find their own answers, while relying on and using their own resources.*
- Coaching requires the coach to actively listen to the coachee and ask appropriate powerful questions (direct, short/simple, challenging/thought-provoking, open-ended, probing, asked with genuine care and curiosity, future-directed, and solution-oriented) that will help the coachee come up with the solution themselves. It requires the coach to:
    - Be genuinely curious
    - Create learning opportunities
    - Generate inspired action
    - Be truly present and engage in truly focused/global listening – the coachee's thoughts, feelings, emotions, words (said/unsaid), action, inaction, interaction, intuition
    - Focus attention on, trust, and respect the coachee
    - Trust the process
- Coaching is most effectively and appropriately used when there is low to moderate risk/urgency.
- Coaching is NOT about the coach solving the coachee's problems. It's not primarily about improving performance, attaining goals or achieving results, although all of this will happen over time, along with:
    - Increased self-confidence
    - Increased self-awareness and emotional intelligence
    - Improved ability to manage time and stress

THE GROW COACHING MODEL

The GROW model is the simplest and most widely-used coaching framework:

G – Goal	R - Reality	O – Options / Alternatives	W – Wrap-Up & Way Forward
5% of your time	5% of your time	80% of your time	10% of your time
• What do you want to get out of this session? • How would you know that the time had been well spent? What feeling would you like to have at the end of this session? • What is the most productive thing we could do in the session?	• What has happened since the last session or meeting? • What are the key factors here? • On a scale of 1 to 10, how severe / serious / fabulous is the situation? • What is happening in your life/ in the team/ in the organization at the moment? • What's working? What's not working? • What needs to change?	• What is the full range of possible actions in this circumstance? • Which is the most attractive to me/us now? • What are the costs and benefits of taking this action? • If you are experiencing a problem with your goals: • Are there times when the problem doesn't occur? • What is different about these times? • How can I/we do more about these times? • How have I/ we stopped the problem from being completely overwhelming? What has worked for me/us in the past?	Before you end the session you need to plan what you are going to do next. So ... • List some specific tasks • List who is going to do what • List some people who can support you • What sort of things might stop you being successful? • How will you know if you are being successful? • What will you do if you find these things are getting in the way?

G – Goal	R - Reality	O – Options / Alternatives	W – Wrap-Up & Way Forward
		<ul><li>What can be done to change the situation?</li><li>How can I/we move towards the goal?</li><li>Who can support me/us in making the change?</li><li>What are the costs and benefits of this course of action?</li></ul>	

 For a deeper dive on the GROW Model, check out the source work of Sir John Whitmore (see the *Sources & Additional Resources* section).

During the coaching process, you will inevitably come up with some really insightful questions that will create breakthroughs for your coachees. You may not even realize you're doing this, while being in flow. Here are some powerful coaching questions you may consider using to get your coachee unstuck and on their way to their own epiphanies:

STARTING THE SESSION

What's on the top of your mind?
What's happened since we last spoke?
What would you like to talk about?
What's new/the latest/the update?
How was your week?
Where are you right now?
What would you like to work on today?

ASSESSMENT

What do you make of it?
What do you think is best?
How does it look to you?
How do you feel about it?
What resonates for you?
What is the opportunity here?
What is the challenge?
How does this fit with your plans/way of life/values?
What do you think that means?
What is your assessment?
What else might be going on here?

CLARIFICATION

What do you mean?
What does it feel like to you?
What is the part that is not yet clear?
Say more.
What do you want?
What are some examples?

ELABORATION

Tell me more.
What else?
What other ideas / thoughts / feelings do you have about it?

EXPLORATION

What is here that you want to explore?
What part of the situation have you not yet explored?
What other angles can you think of?
What is just one more possibility?
What are your other options?
What is possible?
What if it works out exactly as you want it to?
What is the ideal state/outcome?
What is exciting to you about this?
What does your intuition tell you?

HISTORY

What caused it?
What led up to it?
What have you tried so far?
What do you make of it all?
How has that worked out for you?
When have you encountered something like this before?

INTEGRATION

What will you take away from this?
How do you explain this to yourself?
What was the lesson?
How will you make sure you remember what you learned?
How will you pull this all together?
How will you apply this in the future?

LEARNING

What would you do …
… if your life depended on taking action?
… if you had free choice in the matter?
… if the same thing came up again?
… if we could wipe the slate clean?
… if you had to do it all over again?

OPTIONS

What are the possibilities?
If you had your choice, what would you do?
What are the possible solutions?
What will happen if you do? If you don't?
What options can you create?

OUTCOMES

What do you want?
What is your desired outcome?
If you got it, what would you have?
How will you know you have reached it?
What would it look like?

PERSPECTIVE
When you are 100 years old, what will you want to say about your life?
What will you think about this 5 years from now?
How does this relate to your life purpose?
In the bigger scheme of things, how important is this?
So what?

PLANNING / STRATEGY
What do you plan to do about it?
What is your game plan?
What kind of plan do you need to create?
How could you improve the situation?
Now what?
How does this fit within the larger ecosystem?
What are the broader implications?

PREDICTIONS
How do you suppose it will all work out?
What will that get you?
Where will this lead?
What are the chances of success?
What is your prediction?

RESOURCES
What resources do you need to help you decide?
What do you know about it now?
How can you find out more about it?
What kind of picture do you have right now?
What resources are available to you?
Who else can do this instead of you?
For whom could this be a development opportunity? For whom else?

RETROSPECTIVE
If you could do it over again, what would you do differently?
If it had been you, what would you have done?
How else could this be handled?
If you could do anything you wanted, what would you do?

SUBSTANCE
What seems to be the trouble/issue/challenge?
What seems to be the main obstacle?
What is stopping you?
What concerns you most about ...?
What do you want?

SUMMARY
What is your conclusion?
How is this working for you?
How would you describe this?
What do you think this all amounts to?
How would you summarize the effort so far?

TAKING ACTION, DRIVING ACCOUNTABILITY
What action will you take? By when? And after that?
What will you do? By when?
What action is needed now?
Where do you go from here?
When will you do that?
What are your next steps?
By what date or time will you complete them?
What is the action plan?
What do you have to do to get the job done?
What support do you need to accomplish it?

Situational Leadership – The situation and employee's lifecycle stage determine which style you as a manager will use with your team members. Employees will require different leadership styles from you at different points of their careers. As a leader and manager, you must learn to use all four styles and recognize when to apply them appropriately:

EMPLOYEE LIFECYCLE POINT / DEVELOPMENT LEVEL	MANAGER STRATEGY/STYLE	SUMMARY	TEAM PHASE CORRELATE
D1 – Low Competence & High Commitment	S1: DIRECTING (High Directive & Low Supportive) Help them build up their confidence through: Acknowledging their transferable skills and commitment Providing direction to them Frequent check-ins with them	D1: When employees start a new role, they are open to and require more direction (S1) from their managers	Forming
D2 – Low-Some Competence & Low Commitment	S2: COACHING (High Directive & High Supportive) Re-energize and re-teach them by: Exploring their concerns and encouraging them Explaining the why to them Redirecting and re-teaching them Involving them in problem-solving	D2: When employees have been in role long enough to develop more competence (and may have become more disenchanted), they are open to and require more Coaching (S2) from their managers	Storming

EMPLOYEE LIFECYCLE POINT / DEVELOPMENT LEVEL	MANAGER STRATEGY/STYLE	SUMMARY	TEAM PHASE CORRELATE
D3 – Moderate – High Competence & Variable Commitment	S3: SUPPORTING (Low Directive & High Supportive) Build up their confidence in their competence and abilities by: Asking them for their inputs Listening to and encouraging them Facilitating problem-solving via open-ended questioning	D3: As employees become even more competent in their role, they need more Supportive (S3) behaviors from their managers	Norming
D4 – High Competence & High Commitment	S4: DELEGATING (Low Directive & Low Supportive) Value their contributions by: Acknowledging their expertise Supporting their autonomy Encouraging them to innovate and to continue learning	D4: Experts in role can be Delegated to (S4)	Performing

 For a deeper dive on Situational Leadership, check out the works of the sources: Ken Blanchard and Paul Hersey (see the *Sources & Additional Resources* section).

OTHER LEADERSHIP STYLES

The four leadership styles highlighted in the Situational Leadership model are not the only ones available to you. Daniel Goleman identified six leadership styles, each one of which has its benefits and drawbacks when used – you guessed it – in different situations. These are:

- Coaching – focused on the individual needs, situations, and aspirations of each of your team members, and developing them for the future. This relates directly to the S2 Coaching style of Situational Leadership.
- Democratic – brainstorming, driving and building consensus so that everyone feels empowered and that they have bought into and are committed to decisions. This comes with the risk of increasing the timelines to accommodate everyone's input and the possibility of unintentionally excluding others' opinions. This assumes that the included employees have experience and knowledge in the area. It should not be used in times of crisis, when time is of the essence. This is a combination of the S2 Coaching and S3 Supporting styles of Situational Leadership.
- Authoritative (not Authoritarian) – inspiring your team members to take action through a compelling vision and personal connection to the organization's mission and strategy. This is found in the S1 Directive style of Situational Leadership.
- Affiliative – friendly, relationship-oriented, supportive, and fostering belonging. Overused, or solely used, this style runs the risk of creating perceptions of favoritism and may interfere with the ability to have effective critical conversations around and take unpopular actions (i.e., performance management conversations, terminations).
- Pacesetting – role modeling and expecting exceptional efforts and quality results, at the risk of taking on too much yourself, burning yourself and others out, and not providing development opportunities for others to learn.

- Coercive – here's where authoritarian comes in – command-and-control, directing and demanding immediate compliance to produce instant results. This style is most effective in short-term, immediate crisis/critical/emergency situations, but is not recommended for creating long-term, sustainable psychologically-safe environments where people feel comfortable to stay, learn, and grow. This (along with Authoritative) is related to the S1 Directive style of Situational Leadership.

These six styles are presented in this order to emphasize the formula most likely to yield positive, productive, and sustainable results. Daniel Goleman recommends leveraging Coaching, Democratic, and Authoritative leadership styles as your dominant focus, with a sprinkle – but not too much – of Affiliative. The Pacesetting and Coercive styles have their place and time as well, but are not sustainable, long-term solutions, as they are most likely to create hostile and toxic work environments.

For a deeper dive on these six styles, check out the work of Daniel Goleman, considered to be the seminal and prolific expert in emotional intelligence (see *Sources & Additional Resources* section).

As you compare the four Situational Leadership styles to Daniel Goleman's six leadership styles, you will note that the former are really a combination of the latter. This supports the mindset of *AND*, discussed earlier, and invites leaders to integrate the styles together to match the needs of each specific situation. These two models are, indeed, complementary. To determine which leadership style is the most effective for any given situation, you will need to keep attuned to the changing capabilities and needs of each of your team members. Leverage your check-ins and one-on-ones, discussed in Chapter 6, to do so. Practice flexing into each of the styles and, soon enough, it will become second nature!

Now that you are familiar with the Situational Leadership model, which applies to individuals, you might find it interesting that that a very similar model, which actually preceded it, can be used with teams! Tuckman's much-touted "Stages of Group Development" model can be easily seen progressing in this sequence as well. All groups/teams go through this cycle:

1. Forming – the honeymoon period where team members excitedly get together with grand aspirations of what they will accomplish working together
2. Storming – jockeying for power, who will lead, whose ideas will be implemented
3. Norming – rules of engagement are identified and adopted and team roles are clarified, enabling a calmer and more orderly approach to the team's work
4. Performing – the team is able to operate smoothly, with minimal distractions and unproductive conflict

As a team lead, it is important for you to recognize this sequence, identify where your team is, and provide the appropriate guidance and support needed at each stage, to help them to progress to the next one. Keep in mind that any disruption to the system (a new team member, loss of a team member, new processes, new systems, a new leader, etc.) will set the team back to a previous stage to work through those issues again, and develop new team agreements.

 For a deeper dive on the Stages of Team Development, check out the source work of Bruce Tuckman (see the *Sources & Additional Resources* section).

SELF: What is your comfort level in being able to coach your team members? Are you receiving coaching from your boss or other internal/external resources? How explicit have you made your expectations around this? How easy is it for you to identify when a team member is at a different point in their employee lifecycle and know when – and flex to – another leadership style (that) might be more effective? Which are your preferred, go-to leadership styles? Which are your least preferred? How can and will you develop all of these skills and different leadership styles to become an even more effective manager and leader?

TEAM: What are your team members' explicit expectations around receiving coaching for themselves? From whom? You? Colleagues/teammates? Other internal/external resources? Are they interested in coaching their peers? How can and will you find out? How can and will you help them develop these coaching skills?

ORGANIZATION: What are your organization's explicit expectations of your role in coaching? What resources are available to you to help you develop your coaching skills? Are there internal coaches available to employees of your organization? Are external executive coaches being utilized?

REALITY CHECK: Is your organization investing in upskilling its employees in coaching? Who receives coaching in your organization? Is it available to your executives? A select group of leaders? The entire organization? How can and will you influence the availability and accessibility of coaching for all who want it within your organization?

CHAPTER 9

FEEDBACK & CRITICAL CONVERSATIONS

"Can I give you some feedback?" Let's be real – no one ever says that when they're about to compliment you about something; if they have something positive to say, they would just come out and say it. And it immediately puts most recipients on the defensive, fearing that they did something wrong and let others down. We need to develop a feedback-rich culture, where feedback is provided on a regular basis (not just when something goes wrong) and is meaningful and action-able for future success, rather than dredging up the past.

Some truths about effective feedback and best practices:

- Providing feedback is a management non-negotiable.
- On-going feedback is an expectation and practice within strong, productive, and effective company cultures – where it is welcomed and asked for, provided at the end of each appropriate endpoint (end of a meeting, completion of a task/sprint/project/presentation, etc.).
- Positive feedback is most effectively provided when it is witnessed, in public (during prescribed "after action reviews" in team meetings, if the employee is OK with that) and in private (during check-ins and one-on-ones).
- Constructive and developmental feedback is most effec-tively provided as soon after the event as feasible, in a pri-vate setting, ONLY on what you, yourself, have witnessed/ experienced. (Should someone come to you to provide feedback on one of your team members, push back and

ask them to provide it to the team member themselves, if you were not present during the incident in question).

- Feedback is a part of everyday operations and NOT a special event. No one should be surprised at any developmental feedback provided during a performance review, as prior conversations about this will have taken place throughout the year.
- It is the responsibility of every manager to know how each of their team members prefers to receive feedback, and to create and maintain a "contract" on how feedback will be communicated both ways (feedback from manager to team member, feedback from team member to manager). Feel free to use the *Explicit Expectations Engagement & Alignment Guide* at the end of this book for this purpose.

Many different feedback tools and models exist. Here are a few from which you can choose … or avoid:

SBI – SITUATION | BEHAVIOR | IMPACT | INTENT

The SBI feedback model is a Center for Creative Leadership framework for providing constructive feedback that is clear, specific, and actionable. It can help to reduce defensiveness and promote positive change.

- Situation: The context – the specific event/circumstance – in which the behavior occurred, presented as specific and factually as possible, including time, place, and other relevant details, as observed first-person, devoid of generalizations and personal opinions.
- Behavior: The specific behavior on which you are providing feedback, described in a factual and objective manner – mirroring back the behavior, actions that were observed, what was said – without judgment or interpretation. The focus is on the behavior, NOT the person.

- Impact: The effect that the behavior had on others. It can be positive, negative, and/or neutral. The impact can be on you, the team, or the organization as a whole.
- Intent: Identification, through a lens of genuine curiosity and openness, of the person's original intent in that situation.

Note: Be open to receiving feedback, yourself.

The original SBI Model didn't include the more recently-added "Intent" component. This is a more inclusive addition, as it opens the door to more of a two-way conversation around this. Also, the original model called for the use of "When you …" statements in the "Situation" description, which was often received defensively when the feedback was more constructive and corrective in nature. To prevent this, you may instead consider trying out a variation and asking the person how *they* think the specific event went. They may have already realized through their own self-awareness, during or after the fact, that there may have been a misstep or misunderstanding and may already be self-critical and self-punishing. Feeling reprimanded on top of it may exacerbate the situation, unnecessarily. If it becomes apparent that they are not self-aware of how their behavior was received and perceived, then you can ease into the next steps of the model.

Furthermore, to make your feedback even more effective, consider Marshall Goldsmith's feed*forward* method, where the focus is on future success, asking others what they want to change, providing future-focused options/solutions, expanding possibilities, and creating a specific development plan rather than just dwelling on past missteps.

You may have heard – or even experienced – another feedback method called the Feedback/Praise/Compliment Sandwich, where you commend a positive behavior, present the constructive feedback, and end with another positive behavior. It's human nature for recipients of this type of feedback to ignore the positives and only focus on the negative ... and when this method becomes the norm, recipients often feel that the positives (and the people relaying them) are disingenuous. Choose wisely – there are better options.

BEST PRACTICES

GIVING FEEDBACK	RECEIVING FEEDBACK
• Select a private setting without distractions • Be explicit about your care for the recipient and your intent to help them be successful • Use a calm tone, slow pace, and provide space for the recipient to process and ask questions • Be specific • Speak for yourself and what you saw/experienced • Identify your contribution to the situation/issue (if any) and your wish to resolve it • Avoid providing advice, unless asked for • Invite the recipient's response • Steer the conversation into a development plan • Ask for feedback on you	• Stay calm and use a growth mindset, preventing getting defensive • Listen and use clarifying questions and paraphrasing to ensure greater understanding • Ask for advice/options on how to handle similar situations in the future, including creating a development plan to do so • Say "Thank you"

For a deeper dive into the SBI Model, check out the Center for Creative Leadership at www.ccl.org. Check out, too, the source work of Susan Scott (see the *Sources & Additional Resources* section).

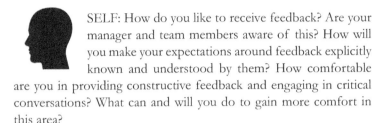

SELF: How do you like to receive feedback? Are your manager and team members aware of this? How will you make your expectations around feedback explicitly known and understood by them? How comfortable are you in providing constructive feedback and engaging in critical conversations? What can and will you do to gain more comfort in this area?

TEAM: How does each of your team members like to receive feedback? Is it different for each of them? How can and will you determine what their explicit expectations are in this area?

ORGANIZATION: What are your organization's explicit expectations of your role in providing feedback to and conducting critical conversations with your team members? What support is provided to you to make this happen?

REALITY CHECK: How is feedback experienced in your organization? Do people receive real feedback, both positive and constructive, in a way that supports their dignity and being respected? Is feedback welcomed or dreaded? Is providing regular feedback built into processes, project stages, and programs or does it happen ad hoc when something bad happens? Is constructive feedback used to help people learn and grow, or is it avoided and used as an excuse and rationale to hold people back in their careers? How can and will you positively impact this? What expectations can and will you make explicit around this?

CHAPTER 10

PERFORMANCE MANAGEMENT

All of the topics we have covered up to this point contribute to the operationalization of performance management. Let's summarize how they all come together and explore how to help any wayward team members get back on track, should they not meet the explicit expectations set forth for them.

Some truths about performance management, when it's done right:

- Encourages employee growth and development
- Motivates employees to take their performance to the next level
- Is an ongoing process, not just an annual event
- Performance discussions focus on behaviors and competencies that will improve performance moving forward, rather than only reviewing past actions
- Either managers or employees may initiate dialogue on performance
- Helps employees understand business goals and how their performance impacts them
- Employees take ownership over their own development; managers will support, facilitate, and enable as feasible
- Frequent and recurring one-on-ones and on-going feedback throughout the year prevent any "year-end surprises"
- Performance is directly linked to salary increases and bonus payout
  - In some cases, salary increases for high performers may be limited due to where their salary falls within their role's range (i.e., they may receive a lower percentage salary increase than guidelines state if they

are already above the range's midpoint and/or close to the top of the range).

- In other cases, employees who are far below their role's compensation range's midpoint may receive a higher percentage salary increase in an attempt to get them closer to midpoint, if they receive a satisfactory or above performance review rating.
  - To prevent these awkward situations and conversations (and possible result of employee dissatisfaction, disengagement, and regrettable turnover), review your team members' salaries with your Human Resources/People & Culture Partner to ensure salary competitiveness within your industry and organization's compensation strategy; make any adjustments necessary separately from the performance management process, as this is not the process's intended purpose

- Employees who do not improve their performance will undergo your organization's Progressive Discipline Process, whereby you, as the team member's manager, will work with the company's Human Resources/People & Culture Business Partner to orchestrate the following:
  - When a performance issue is identified, you, as the employee's manager, will provide verbal feedback and ensure your team member's explicit understanding of the role's performance expectations. Document when you delivered this, what was said, and what was verbally agreed-to.
  - If/when a second or continued occurrence of the same issue is manifested after the "verbal warning," you, as the employee's manager, will deliver a written warning, placing your team member on a Performance Improvement Plan (PIP), repeating explicit performance expectations, and delineating milestones to be achieved within a certain time frame, (recommendation is 1-3 months) to successfully complete the PIP.

- ○ If/when your team member does not meet the explic-
  itly-identified PIP milestones and expectations within
  the designated timeframe, you, as the employee's manager, in partnership with your Human Resources/
  People & Culture Business Partner, will terminate your
  team member's employment with your organization.
- ○ Note that some organizations add a "suspension"
  phase between the written warning and the termination as another opportunity for the employee to turn
  around their performance (this may be especially true
  in unionized environments). Check with your organization to confirm your policy and process on PIPs to
  ensure consistency and equity in employee treatment.

SELF: What is your comfort level in engaging in performance management? How are you experiencing it
from your boss? What can and will you do to increase
your confidence and effectiveness in this area?

TEAM: What are your team members' expectations
around their performance management? How confident
are they in its use, validity, fairness, and effectiveness?
How involved and empowered are team members in providing feedback to their teammates and having a say in accountability, ratings,
and payouts? How well do they understand the explicit performance
expectations of their roles? What can and will you do to ensure this
and that there are no surprises?

ORGANIZATION: What are your organization's
explicit expectations of your role around performance
management? What support is provided to you to make
this happen?

REALITY CHECK: Are performance management discussions looked forward to in your organization and seen as a productive and impactful way to ensure that each and every employee is contributing their fair share and being recognized appropriately and equitably, or are they met with eye-rolls, sarcasm, skepticism, negative attitudes, and seen as an annual "check-the-box" exercise that is not perceived as equitable or impactful? How well does your organization's performance management system and process work? What do other managers and your team members say about it? What can and will you do to optimize its effectiveness? If your organization uses a rating system, how fair is it perceived as being? Are you required to force-fit your team members into a bell curve for performance and assign rating that way, or are you free to provide whichever ratings are truly earned and deserved by them? Does it engage or disengage employees? What can and will you do to influence the development and use of an effective and motivational performance management process?

CHAPTER 11

ENGAGING & MOTIVATING YOUR TEAM

Year-after-year, Gallup polls consistently report that only about 37% of employees are actively engaged in their work. Research also shows that when employees do choose to leave on their own, they tend to leave because of their manager, not the company.

To avoid "regrettable turnover" (the loss of valuable employees who you would prefer to keep and grow within the organization), people leaders have myriad tools available to them, including:

- Stay interviews
- Check-ins and one-on-ones
- Team-building tools to help understand employee motivations, communication styles, feedback and recognition preferences, etc.

FOUNDATIONAL PHILOSOPHY

The foundation for all of this is the Platinum Rule, introduced at the beginning of this book. Recall that most people unconsciously abide by "The Golden Rule" ("treat others the way you want to be treated") because it's what they've been taught in school, by religion, and even in commercials. The reality, though, is that The Golden Rule presupposes that everyone is exactly the same, with the same backgrounds, ability levels, education, ideologies, etc. As we know, that is not true - the world, as any organization, is comprised of diverse individuals with diverse backgrounds, skillsets, worldviews, etc. which we need to tap into and honor if we are to successfully accomplish our mission. And different people have different needs, motivations, and aspirations, of which we are unaware unless we ASK them through relationship-building. And that is the Platinum Rule: "Treat others the way *THEY* want to be treated." Of course, this must abide by certain parameters of what is feasible, possible, legal, fair, just, and aligns with the organization's values. Team-building tools and frameworks like DiSC, Myers-Briggs Type Indicator, and the Enneagram help to identify areas of sameness and differentiation, so that team members get to understand themselves and each other better, and work more effectively together.

One area of differentiation may be in terms of interpersonal dynamics and communication styles. Different employees prefer and are more responsive to a variety of communication styles. Ask your team members to rank-order their preferred mode or combination of modes and capture this on the *Explicit Expectations Engagement & Alignment Guide* (see Chapter 17):

- Be Brief, Be Bright, Be Gone: fast-paced and to-the-point
- Include/Involve Me: motivational/inspiring, relationship-focused
- Show me that you care: patient, relaxed
- Give me ALL the details: factual and to-the-point

 For a deeper dive on this, check out the source work of William Moulton Marston on the DiSC system (see the *Sources & Additional Resources* section).

CONTINUOUSLY MOTIVATING YOUR TEAM

When seeking to ensure that you are effectively focusing on the right ways to continuously motivate your team, remember that individuals become engaged by different drivers, some of which will be of more primary importance, including:

1. Alignment of their own values to the leader's and the organization's, especially around fairness, integrity, and excellence
2. Being recognized for the help and contributions they are making to the team/organization
3. Being recognized and rewarded for their achievements; being considered the best in a specific area
4. Being recognized for their uniqueness and creative talents; alignment with purpose
5. Acquiring knowledge, wisdom, and mastery so as not to look foolish
6. Being safe, comfortable, and secure, especially by belonging to a "tribe" and working for a trusted leader
7. Opportunities for growth, expansion, and pursuing fun, new experiences
8. Control and autonomy over themselves, their team, their work
9. Peaceful, harmonious, and collaborative environments, free of conflict, where everyone is treated equitably

 For a deeper dive on this, check out my other business book, *The How and Why: Taking Care of Business with the Enneagram* (see the *Sources & Additional Resources* section).

People managers who take the time and effort to determine which of these is of most importance to each of their team members, and apply the Platinum Rule to treat them the way *THEY* want to be treated (with the previously-mentioned caveats), will reap the benefits of a motivated, engaged, and satisfied workforce. And when you take the extra step to integrate these perspectives into your own (invoking the Rhodium Rule discussed earlier), you will see that it becomes even easier and you become even more effective as a manager, leader, employee, and human being (and yes, this will positively impact your personal life, too!).

REWARDS & RECOGNITION

When it comes to rewarding and recognizing your team members, you have the traditional channels available to you that most people focus on: their salaries and annual increases, bonuses, stock and equity options. It is important to also remind your team members of the organization's investment in them in others areas as well:

- The value of their medical benefits – how much does the organization cover on their behalf that they don't have to pay?
- Any 401(k) match? Are they taking advantage of the maximum company match? That's free money!!!
- Healthcare spending accounts can provide them with a pre-tax benefit and save them around 30% on some of their medical expenses
- How much is their Paid Time Off worth? Including Holidays and Shutdowns?
- How much are their stock options and long-term incentive plans potentially worth?
- Commuter incentives
- Tuition reimbursement

What other creative, no-/low-cost options do you have available to you?

What do your employees value? More time off? Attendance at conferences? The ability to pursue a passion project? Coffee? Time with you? Time with the organization's leadership? A nice dinner or weekend away with their partner, especially if they've been putting in long hours for a special work project/deliverable? The ability to work from home more? Fresh-baked chocolate chip cookies, made by you? A quieter/larger work space? Personalized, hand-written "thank you" cards? Shout-outs in team or all hands meetings? A note from your boss to them? Testimonials from customers? Mentorship opportunities (as either a mentor or a mentee)? Something else?

You will face organizational and system constraints in providing compensation-related rewards to your employees, AND you can and will still be able to find creative, fun, and customized ways to show them that they are valued, that you recognize their efforts and achievements, and that you care about them. If you're still in doubt about what is important to them and would make them feel recognized and appreciated, ask them!

CONDUCT STAY INTERVIEWS REGULARLY

In conjunction with check-ins, the Stay Interview is a proven way to get to understand the needs of each of your team members, including how they prefer to feel recognized and appreciated. Using the information gleaned from them, you can customize the way you interact with, motivate, and reward your team members, while ensuring that the team and organization are benefitting from their input, and each team member is feeling energized and satisfied by the work that they do. Incorporate these into every possible opportunity of interaction, including during:

- The recruiting and interview process
- Orientation/On-Boarding
- Times of Turnover (remaining employees may follow coworkers to their new employers)
- Career and Development Discussions
- Follow-up on engagement survey results
- Recognition of a job particularly well-done (what was it about that that so engaged them?)
- Goal-setting
- Check-ins – Consider making the "Stay Interview" a recurring topic of your check-ins (perhaps revisited quarterly

or when you feel there is a need to do so – like seeing a change in behavior or output).

- When you sense that something is off (reduction in performance/output, change in attitude/mood, diminished socialization, etc.).
    - Recognize: See Something – pay attention to the (sometimes subtle) changes
    - Verbalize: Say Something – let the team member you noticed and care
    - Mobilize: Do Something – explore available options and co-create a solution

Ask whichever of these is most appropriate to the situation (don't ask them all at once!):

- What really matters to you?
- What do you like about your work?
- What keeps you here?
- What makes for a great day at work?
- What is something new you would like to learn/do this year?
- What would you like to change about your job?
- What would you like to change about the team/department?
- How can we utilize your talents more fully?
- Which one thing could make your job more satisfying/ rewarding?
- How can you feel better-supported in your career goals?
- How can you be better-recognized? For what?
- What kind of recognition is meaningful to you? Public? Private? Monetary? Other?
- When we frustrate each other or come into conflict with one another, how shall we best resolve it?
- Are you getting what you thought you'd be getting when you joined us?
- What aren't you getting that you did want?

- What wonderful surprises are you getting that you didn't consider?

 For a deeper dive on this, check out the source work of Beverly Kaye (see the *Sources & Additional Resources* section).

 SELF: What motivates you? What drives you? What engages and inspires you? How does your manager know about this? How will you be explicit with your expectations of your manager in knowing how to motivate you more effectively?

 TEAM: What motivates each of your team members? How will you determine how each one is best engaged and rewarded? What can and will you do to ensure that each of your team members feels motivated, engaged, and energized?

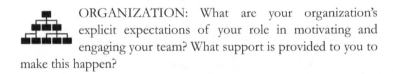 ORGANIZATION: What are your organization's explicit expectations of your role in motivating and engaging your team? What support is provided to you to make this happen?

REALITY CHECK: How much energy is devoted by your organization to identify how motivated and engaged your workforce is? If/when an annual engagement/satisfaction survey is conducted, how transparent is the leadership in sharing the results? Are employees involved in developing solutions to the issues? Are action plans co-developed between leadership and teams of employees? What happens to leaders of teams who are the most disengaged/dissatisfied? How/are leaders of the most engaged/satisfied teams rewarded? How visible are the actions, if any? What can and will you do to ensure that action is taken on any such surveys (which is the expectation of those who fill it out) so that it doesn't become an activity in which employees lose faith and become even less engaged/satisfied?

CHAPTER 12

EMPLOYEE & CAREER DEVELOPMENT

Some truths about effective career development:

Inevitably, Stay Interviews will lead into a career aspiration conversation. Remember to set and make explicit realistic expectations, according to your organization's philosophy on career development:

- Refer to your organization's tools for individuals (if created and available) to identify explicit expectations and responsibilities for each level in their function/department. Feel free to reference these in your discussions with them, keeping in mind that other factors must also be taken into consideration.
- Tenure does not automatically result in promotions; There must be a real business need to justify a promotion (you can't make everyone a Vice President, even if they're qualified to perform the role – who would take on the other work that needs to be done? How would your organization pay for it? What would it look like in the industry?).
- One's career can be developed along a *ladder* (upward growth) AS WELL as via *lattice* (lateral moves to other functions to gain even greater knowledge of other parts of the organization and how it all fits and works together as a system).
- Each individual is responsible for their own career development and growth. You, as their manager, and the organization are there to enable and support this, as possible.

- Don't assume that each of your team members aspires to a greater leadership role within your function (or even at all) just because that may have been your own path and experience – that's where that pesky, derailing Golden Rule thinking shows up. Individual employee aspirations need to be validated via on-going conversations with them. Employee readiness and willingness to take on additional responsibilities and challenges can change according to what's going on in their personal and professional lives.
- Employees usually need to exhibit "Meets Expectations" (or whatever nomenclature your organization uses that equates to this) or above performance review ratings for the past several years (in organizations that conduct performance reviews) and/or be considered to have "high potential" (where the organization sees a runway for them for future roles, ideally with already-held conversations about their own interests and aspirations for them).

If/when a team member shares an aspiration to become a people manager (which may not be feasible in the foreseeable future due to your organization's structure, growth strategy, the employee's readiness, etc.), explore with them these options/potential opportunities and ask them to consider:

- Volunteering to lead projects or teams or take on an interim role to cover for another employee's leave of absence. Even if there are no formal management positions available, leadership skills can still be developed by volunteering to lead projects or teams, providing the chance to develop coaching and people management skills and to motivate and inspire others.
- Taking on mentoring or coaching roles. Participating in your organization's mentoring program as a mentor and/ or mentee. This is a great way to share knowledge and experience with others, and it can also help them develop leadership skills.

- Becoming a subject matter expert in an area important to your organization's strategy. This provides them with the opportunity to build and share knowledge with others, and it can also lead to more leadership opportunities.
- Getting involved in company culture initiatives to promote your organization's values. This is a great way for them to develop and demonstrate leadership skills, gain visibility to leadership, and make a positive impact on your organization.
- Networking with other managers. Talking to other managers within your organization and/or your organization's industry to learn about their experiences and get advice on how to develop more leadership skills. This is a great way for them to gain insights and learn from others with similar career aspirations to find out about their personal path.

CAREER DEVELOPMENT PLANS

Co-create a Career Development Plan based on a team member's aspirations, ensuring that it is a combination of:

- Education: 10 – 20% of time/resources allocated to baseline/foundational knowledge gathering through coursework, etc.
- Exposure: 20 – 30 % of time/resources allocated to feedback, coaching, mentoring, observing others who already have the targeted skill
- Experiences: 60 – 70% of time/resources should be allocated to opportunities for practical application of the new skills/knowledge on the job

EMPLOYEE: _____ **ROLE | TITLE:** _____

	KNOWLEDGE | SKILL | ABILITY | EXPERIENCE TO BE DEVELOPED (Be Specific.)	DEVELOPMENT ACTIVITY List realistic Actions to take to achieve this objective, incorporating: 10–20% Education/Foundational Casswork 30–30% Exposure/Being mentored/coached 60–70% Experiential/On-the-Job	METRIC(S) & MEASURE(S)s OF SUCCESS	RESOURCES | SUPPORT NEEDED	MILESTONE(S) & TARGET COMPLETION DATE(S)	STATUS UPDATE
CURRENT ROLE						
FUTURE ROLE						

	SIGNATURE	DATE
EMPLOYEE:		
MANAGER:		

Revisit each of your team member's career development plan regularly with them to verify progress, validate focus, see where you can help, and make any changes necessary.

SELF: What are your expectations around your own career development at your organization? What aspirations and timelines do you have for yourself? Have you made these expectations explicit to your boss? What kind of support and opportunities for development are they providing for you? What introductions and doors are they opening for you? Which others do you want and how will you let them know?

TEAM: What are each of your team members' aspirations and interests for growth and development? How often/soon do they expect to be promoted? Why do they have this expectation? How do you know this? What have they told you about their explicit expectations around their career development? How aware is each of them about *their* role in their own career development? What are their expectations around your and the organization's role in their career development? How can and will you ensure that their explicit expectations are known by you and that they know what is actually possible?

ORGANIZATION: What resources does your organization have to support career development? How is succession planning conducted at your organization? How valid is it based on real data and having explicit conversations with the employees on the succession plan? How can and will you make a positive impact in this area?

REALITY CHECK: What are your organization's stories around career development and advancement? What are the metrics around internal promotions versus external hires when opportunities present themselves? What is the ideal mix, per your company's culture and strategy? When an opportunity opens up, how are candidates selected for consideration? Is there an open call with a posted job requisition? Are people appointed, without job postings, interviews, or consideration of other candidates? How does that impact morale of the current workforce? How does your organization invest in the development of its employees? Is there a tuition reimbursement program? Are employees encouraged to identify and pursue training opportunities like certifications? Is there reimbursement for professional association membership? How well-publicized and easy-to-access are these? To whom are they made available? Is there a fair and equitable process that is consistently used in filling new vacancies, especially those for which there may be multiple viable internal candidate options? What can and will you do to make a positive impact in this area?

CHAPTER 13

EFFECTIVE TEAM MEETINGS

We've all been in meetings (and seen memes about them) that "could have been an email." Nothing disenchants, frustrates, and disengages busy people than feeling like their time is being wasted. And you don't want to gain a reputation of having ineffective meetings, where people are dreading being there and/or multi-tasking. When you're considering scheduling a meeting or pondering if that's the best medium for your purpose, use the rubric below to ensure that it is, indeed, necessary, and when an alternate communication and interaction medium might be more appropriate.

MEDIUM	PURPOSE / CONSIDERATIONS
1:1 Text/ SMS	Is the information brief and doesn't require a lot of thought? Is the information personal and/or sensitive? Do you need to receive a response right away?
1:1 / Group E-Mail	Is the information straightforward and doesn't require discussion/clarification? Is the information time-sensitive? Do you want/need a written record of the communication?
1:1 Call	Is the information complex and/or requires clarification? Do you need to build rapport or relationships? Is the communication time-sensitive? Is the information personal and/or sensitive? Have multiple emails been sent on this topic without resolution?
Group Meeting	Is there a need for discussion and collaboration? Do you need to brainstorm ideas, solve a problem, get everyone on the same page, or make a decision? Is there a lot of information to share that may result in questions/need for clarification from the recipients? Do you need to build rapport or relationships?

Effective meetings must have an agenda sent out at least 24 (ideally 48) hours before the meeting's start, so that team members can:

- know its purpose and expected results/outcomes and decide if it's necessary for them to attend, delegate it to someone more appropriate, and/or invite (an)other expert attendee(s)
- prepare for it
- rearrange their calendars and schedules, if necessary

Effective agendas include:

- Logistics (Date/Start Time – End Time/Location, if breakfast/lunch will be provided if during those hours)
- Meeting's Overall Topic and Objective(s)
- Attendees and their roles (i.e., who is running the meeting, the organizational roles/functions represented by each attendee)
- A specific listing of: Time, Topic of Discussion, Expected Outcome, and Topic Leader
- An opportunity at the beginning to ground/focus, check-in, review purpose and ground rules, etc.
- A closure where decisions/agreements and accountability are reviewed/clarified and feedback is provided

BEST PRACTICES:

- Start on time with any necessary introductions, ground rules, ice-breakers/check-ins/presencing/inclusion exercise, and reiteration of the purpose of the meeting
  - To prevent people from being late, consider scheduling and starting your meeting at 5-15 minutes past the hour, so that people have time to commute or take a break between their previous meetings
- Ensure that all participants' voices and input are heard, even if some need time to process and provide it later that day/week for inclusion/consideration

- End on time (ideally allowing for participants to have a quick break before their next meeting/time to get there) with decisions, next steps, and accountabilities clearly defined
- Include an opportunity for feedback on the meeting's effectiveness and success, and consideration for future iterations

---

 SELF: What meetings do you look forward to attending or leading? Which do you dread? Why? Do you need to be in every meeting that is on your calendar? To whom might you be able to delegate some of your meeting attendance (who may experience it as a development opportunity)? Are there other meetings you *should* be in to help you be more effective in your role and/or provide information, input, and insight only you have? What are your manager's expectations around your attendance at meetings? How do you know? What can and will you do to align your meeting attendance to your and your manager's explicit needs and expectations? What can and will you do to ensure that the right meetings are happening in the most efficient way? What can and will you do to ensure that you're attending the right meetings for your effectiveness and success?

TEAM: What are each of your team members' expectations around participating, being included, heard, and supported in meetings? How do they feel about your team meetings? How comfortable is each of them in offering up a different viewpoint or perspective in meetings? Do they feel encouraged to do so, or fear retribution? How often do they feel shut down? How do you know this? What can and will you do to determine each of their needs and expectations in this area and agree on a way to be reminded should their needs and expectations not be met?

ORGANIZATION: What are your organization's explicit expectations of your role in leading and attending meetings? What resources exist to help and support you in making meetings more effective? Is there a standard practice or expectation around starting 5 minutes late and ending 5 minutes early for meetings requiring in-person attendance, to provide attendees with a buffer to get from their previous or to their next meeting? Are breaks encouraged every 90 minutes for longer meetings? How are people who are absent or late treated? (How) are they brought up to speed on what they missed? What can and will you do to positively impact your organization's meeting culture, making meetings as effective and efficient as possible?

 REALITY CHECK: How much time do you spend in meetings? What about your peers and colleagues? What is the Return on Investment (ROI) of your meeting attendance? What can and will do to increase that ROI?

CHAPTER 14

CHANGE MANAGEMENT

Here are some truths about Change:

- Change is the only constant. We all live and operate in a VUCA (Volatile, Uncertain, Complex, Ambiguous) world, in increasingly competitive environments; as such, you must be vigilant about continuously scanning your environment and competitive landscape to anticipate and plan for future trends and challenges – and adapt your strategy to match.
- There is no longer an expectation of "refreezing" into a new normal after a change has occurred. You must be comfortable with continuous change upon change, and reference your organization's strategy and corporate goals as your and your team's true north for direction.
- Your people will have varying degrees of comfort with change and agility/adaptability to changes. As leaders, you must recognize at which stage each of your team members is, and patiently and caringly support them in getting to the next step, keeping in mind that you may be well ahead of them on the change/loss curve.
- Each manager and leader at your organization is responsible for relaying consistent messaging about and supporting your strategy and any changes you undergo.

When facing change, as people progress through the change/loss curve, they need Information, Empathy, an outlet for their Ideas, and Appreciation. When engaging with team members undergoing a change:

1. Know your purpose
2. Understand and adapt to the person and the situation (e.g., consider cultural differences, DEI), where they are on the change/loss curve, etc.
3. Communicate your message openly, directly, and completely, ending with a question about them and where/how they are
4. Practice active listening
5. Identify where the person is in their personal transition and respond appropriately:

STAGE	MANAGER ACTION	HOW?
Denial	Inform	Provide/reiterate the why/who/what/when/where/how
Resistance	Empathize	Be genuine and caring in understanding/validating what they are going through
Exploration	Ideate	Ask team members for their ideas; provide them the opportunity to co-create the future end state, ideally based on the sharing of *their* ideas
Acceptance	Appreciate	Acknowledge them for coming along on the journey and positively contributing to the new outcome

6. Adjust your response accordingly when the person moves to a different transition phase in the change/loss curve

BEST PRACTICE:

Remember to (in this order):

1. Create space/time box a safe container for the team to work through their disappointment/emotional reactions productively and constructively (if not addressed first, it WILL find a way to leak out/explode later in an unproductive way)
2. Brainstorm what *IS* possible, within these new constraints and new reality
3. Co-create and implement the action plan to move forward

To ensure inclusivity of all possible concerns, cover the following topics in your communications:

1. How/why is this the right thing to do (for you, your team, your organization)?
2. How will it impact other areas? What are the potential repercussions on others (colleagues/stakeholders/customers)?
3. How does it support your goals? Is it the most efficient option? How will it affect cost/budget/profitability? How will it make you look (in terms of brand/reputation)?
4. How does this present an opportunity to make/keep your organization unique? How does the solution bring a unique value? Is it elegant?
5. What is the data/research to support that this is the logical action to take?
6. What are your back-up plans if this fails? What are the consequences if this desired outcome isn't achieved or if you don't take any action?
7. How does this allow growth for/in the future? What are your other options? What are the likely positive outcomes?
8. How is this within your scope of authority/purview to control and execute upon?
9. How does this fit within and affect the overall system/organization? How is it sustainable?

For a deeper dive on this, check out my other business book, *The How and Why: Taking Care of Business with the Enneagram* (see the *Sources & Additional Resources* section).

If you notice your team members getting stuck ... take the following prescribed actions:

REACTION	BEHAVIORAL DESCRIPTION	MANAGER'S ACTION
Disengaged	Quit and Stay ("Quiet Quitting")	• Confront the behavior • Identify actions to get them realigned to their purpose, re-committed, and involved again
Disidentified	"I used to be somebody"	• Explore what was valuable in the previous situation/role • Figure out how/if it's possible to obtain this in the new situation/role
Disoriented	"What should I do?"	• Find out and further clarify what the person doesn't understand • Help them to set their priorities
Disenchanted	"Isn't this awful?" Taking on a victim mentality	• Allow them to vent • Summarize their concerns and genuinely acknowledge/validate their feelings • Look for symptoms of one of the other reactions

KEEP IN MIND TO AVOID THESE COMMON PITFALLS:

COMMON PITFALL	INSTEAD ...
• Not sharing how you feel about the change	• share your support of the change
• Imposing non-neutral feelings on others before understanding their reaction, e.g., "I know this is hard for you" or "I am sure you are upset about this"	• ask for their reaction(s) and respond accordingly
• Communicating more information when employees express strong emotional reactions	• validate their emotions and make space for them to work through them
• Immediately engaging employees in conversations about solutions rather than understanding and validating how they are reacting	• ask for their reaction(s) and respond accordingly
• Not knowing how to empathize	• ask open-ended questions with genuine curiosity and caring, listen, and mirror back what you heard
• Assuming employees who respond agreeably have no concerns	• ask for their concerns
• Guessing about unresolved or unknown implications of the change	• admit what is unknown and get back to employees and communicate when more is known/shared/cascaded

For a deeper dive on this, check out the source work of William Bridges (see the *Sources & Additional Resources* section).

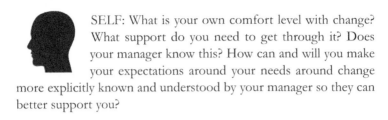 SELF: What is your own comfort level with change? What support do you need to get through it? Does your manager know this? How can and will you make your expectations around your needs around change more explicitly known and understood by your manager so they can better support you?

 TEAM: What are each of your team members' expectations and comfort level with change? How do you know what each of them needs from you during times of change? How can and will you become better aware of their explicit expectations and needs in this arena?

ORGANIZATION: What are your organization's explicit expectations of your role in leading change and managing your team members through change? How do you know? What resources, guidance, and support are available to you?

REALITY CHECK: How well does your organization manage and lead through change? What can and will you do to improve this?

CHAPTER 15

TERMINATIONS

Inevitably, as a people leader you will have to engage in the unpleasant task of terminating an employee. Terminations happen for a variety of reasons:

- Employee's poor performance has not turned around, even after a Performance Improvement Plan
- Egregious behavior, including gross insubordination, theft from the organization, violence/threats, gross negligence, violating company policies, misconduct, damaging property, harassment, falsifying records, excessive absenteeism, drug use, personal use of company property, revealing/selling company trade secrets, breach of confidentiality, lying on their résumé, inappropriate relationships, fraud, bribery, moonlighting at a competitor, etc.
- Job abandonment
- Layoffs due to organizational restructuring and/or financial reasons
- Employee-initiated quitting for personal reasons or professional growth elsewhere

Regardless of reason, an employee exit is a tough situation that has profound implications for all involved – you, the employee, the employee's family and dependents, the team, the organization, etc. For your personal and liability protection, make sure you:

- Partner with your Human Resources/People & Culture representative and Legal department to ensure you are engaging in the organization's defined process, have all the documentation necessary, and treat the employee with consistency and fairness.

- Are objective, treat the employee with respect and dignity, while staying committed to the messaging around the need for the termination.
- In the case of regrettable loss (where you prefer that the employee stays instead of quitting), leave the door open for their return as a boomerang in the future – and if you still have a headcount for them in three months, reach back out to them to see if the opportunity for which they left met their expectations or if they would consider returning.
- If a person is leaving for more money, and you know that they are already being compensated equitably and fairly according to market comparisons, realize that matching the competitor's offer is only a short-term patch – if money is all they're interested in, they will leave the next time an even higher offer is made. And word will (always) get out, making others feel underpaid and setting a precedent that all that someone has to do to make more money is to pro-cure – or bluff about having – another higher-paying offer elsewhere.
- If it's a skill or aspiration mismatch within you department, is there another opportunity with a different department that would be a better match for the employee? This could be a win-win, preventing the need to go through a termi-nation and a costly recruitment process … AND it could serve as a positive example of career movement opportu-nities within the organization.
- Do not badmouth any exiting employee. (This should be a moot (bullet)point since you shouldn't badmouth ANY employee, anyway!).

Terminations and departures will take their toll (emotionally, addi-tional work for remaining others, customer service/experience, etc.) on organizations. And they are a necessary component of the orga-nizational lifecycle. Don't underestimate the emotional toll on you as the deliverer of the news (access the support resources available to you via your manager, the organization, Human Resources/People & Culture, your Employee Wellness/Assistance Program, etc.), and, at the same time, know that not terminating troublesome employees can have many negative organizational consequences and impacts:

- Long-term tolerance, acceptance, or ignoring of behaviors that go against the organization's values send a message to the rest of the organization that the stated culture is not the actual culture; there can be (mis)perceptions of favoritism towards the tolerated party, or even discrimination against the others who are actually performing their jobs well, meeting or exceeding the explicit expectations of the organization/role and within the culture
- The team may feel resentment towards leadership (i.e., you) that doesn't address a low performer/problem issue and creates additional work and stress for them to meet explicit expectations set for the overall team so they don't let down the organization and its customers/stakeholders … and it may lead to poor morale, disengagement, and unproductive behaviors (i.e., "below the line" behaviors like gossiping and complaining)
- The headcount being used for someone who isn't performing or doesn't show they have a passion for being in the role is blocking others within or outside of the organization who actually want to do the job well and could be performing well in it instead

VOLUNTARY TERMINATIONS

The intent of conducting Stay Interviews is to hopefully avoid/prevent regrettable losses and the need to conduct Exit Interviews. However, should an employee decide to depart (and it is a regrettable loss), you have an opportunity to create an "Elegant Exit to get Respectful Returns."

Remind them of the four equities that they are leaving behind that will/ may remain if/when they boomerang back to your organization, that they will now need to build up all over again in the new organization:

1. Social Equity – remind them of making new work colleagues all over again – have you thought about who you're leaving?
2. Influence Equity – relationship- and trust-building starts anew while new leaders and colleagues make up their minds about them
3. Skill Equity – skill deployment differently at new job
4. Financial Equity – stock options, 401(k) matches, etc., long-term incentives, etc.

Attempt re-recruitment with them within 3 - 6 months (the time it takes for employees to realize whether they made a mistake in leaving, if "the grass is not greener"). Reach out to them and ask: "Are you still happy with the decision you made? Want to come back?" This, of course, assumes that you have the headcount and budget to do so, and that it adheres to your organization's policies – as always, check with your Human Resources/People & Culture Business Partner.

For a deeper dive on this, check out the source work of Beverly Kaye (see the *Sources & Additional Resources* section).

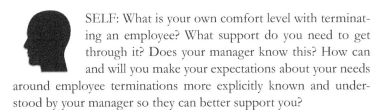

SELF: What is your own comfort level with terminating an employee? What support do you need to get through it? Does your manager know this? How can and will you make your expectations about your needs around employee terminations more explicitly known and understood by your manager so they can better support you?

TEAM: What are each of your team members' expectations when a termination occurs? What do they want to know? What are their concerns? How do you know what each of them needs from you during this type of situation? How will you become better aware of and address their explicit expectations and needs in this arena?

ORGANIZATION: What is your organization's policy and process regarding terminations? What is your organization's policy on boomerang employees (those who want to return after leaving)? How consistently is this applied? What are your organization's explicit expectations of your role in terminations? What resources, guidance, and support are available to you to prepare you for this? What can and will you do to improve on and positively impact this process, if necessary?

REALITY CHECK: What gets communicated to the organization when an employee leaves the organization, voluntarily or involuntarily? How does this communication happen and to whom? How respectful are the communications and how cognizant are they of the recipients' possible concerns and questions? Is it regular practice for your organization to conduct Exit Interviews of departing employees who leave voluntarily? Who collects this data? What is done with it? What actions have been taken to address common themes that are worrisome to the organization? What can and will you do to make improvements in this area?

CHAPTER 16

MANAGING UP

In addition to managing and leading your direct reports and team-mates, in order to be successful in your organization you also need to manage up – to *your* leadership. At the end of each chapter of this book, you were presented with a variety of questions to prompt you to think about yourself, your team members, your organization, and a reality check. Some of these questions already prepared you to manage up, as you started thinking about your expectations and how to make them more explicit to your manager.

What about your manager's expectations of you? What is their preferred communication style? Leadership style? Are you aligned on current, long-term, and changing priorities? What is sacred? What can be deferred? How comfortable are they with you taking initiative on certain things without their knowledge? At what point do they want to get involved or informed? How do they prefer being communicated with? How often? Are certain communications modalities preferred for different reasons? Are there boundaries around time and availability?

What if their boss (skip-level) reaches out to you for something? Does your boss want to be informed/included/involved? Are you making your boss look good to their boss? Are you communicating openly and in advance so that there are no surprises?

How aware are your boss and their boss of your and your team's efforts, results, and challenges? How aware are they of your aspirations and interests? How comfortable are you that they will represent you, your team, and your interests well in performance, compensation, and succession discussions? Do they know about your availability and interest in certain areas that they can delegate to you for development, growth, and visibility? How do they know what obstacles, challenges, and hurdles you face – to achieving your goals or navigating the organization – with which they may be able to help/influence?

How do organizational politics come into play? (Spoiler alert: they do and will in all organizations). With which leaders, teams, and departments can you openly collaborate and play? Which are the ones that need some additional care and insight to navigate?

All of these considerations will help you to understand how you can work with your manager, how you can make their job easier, where you can add value for them and the organization, and how you can be the best and most effective you can be. Wouldn't it be great for each of your team members to also know how to best manage up to you?

Consider using Chapter 17's *Explicit Expectations Engagement & Alignment Guide* with your boss (in addition to using it with each of your team members), so that you are certain about each other's needs and expectations, and support each other's success. The same principles we discussed about your need to be aware of the explicit expectations of your team members are also valid about your manager: they also need to know about your explicit expectations and you need to know theirs.

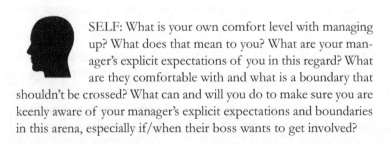

SELF: What is your own comfort level with managing up? What does that mean to you? What are your manager's explicit expectations of you in this regard? What are they comfortable with and what is a boundary that shouldn't be crossed? What can and will you do to make sure you are keenly aware of your manager's explicit expectations and boundaries in this arena, especially if/when their boss wants to get involved?

TEAM: How are each of your team members at managing up to you? To your boss? What are your explicit expectations of each of them in this regard? How can and will you ensure that they know how to manage up to you and any boundaries you have around skip-level involvement?

ORGANIZATION: How do your peers manage up to their bosses? Does the organization's culture support managing up, or are there repercussions? What organizational resources are available to you to help you manage up?

REALITY CHECK: What myths or stories have you heard about people who have managed up and what has happened to them? Are they used as positive, heroic examples to emulate or cautionary tales to avoid? How can and will you positively influence this area? How can and will you find out about, and how to best navigate, your organization's unique political structure?

CHAPTER 17

NEXT STEPS: THE EXPLICIT EXPECTATIONS ENGAGEMENT & ALIGNMENT GUIDE

NOW WHAT?

Now that you've gained a better understanding of what it takes to be an effective and successful people leader, how do you bring it all together in a way that is practical, makes sense, and can serve as a driver and guide to remind and focus you on the Explicit Expectations you and your team members – and any stakeholder – have of yourselves and each other.

Step 1: Find a mutually-convenient time for you and your team member to meet 1:1 to co-create the *Explicit Expectations Engagement & Alignment Guide*. Dedicate 45 – 60 minutes to complete the form together.

Step 2: Ask your team member to recall (or find) your organization's Vision, Mission, and Values. Populate them in the appropriate fields on the Guide. Consider adding these to each of your e-mail signature lines for easier recall and focus.

Step 3: Review the organization's overall goals for the identified period they've been made. Add them to the appropriate field on the Guide. Break them down into what that means for your specific team for the quarter and for this month's focus. Document them in the appropriate fields on the Guide.

Step 4: Agree on and document how often, for how long, and when you will schedule your ongoing 1:1s to take place.

Step 5: Discuss and agree on how performance feedback will be collected on your team member, from whom, and when/how often. Document this agreement on the Guide.

Step 6: Discuss your team member's preferences for recognition and how they prefer to receive it. Document this on the Guide.

Step 7: Ask for and validate your team member's career aspirations, as of this point in time. Where do they seem themselves in the organization? How long from now? Does this seem viable to you? Land on what makes sense at this point in time, given your team member's situation, knowledge, skills, abilities, role and your organization's current state, organization structure, and needs. Document this in the appropriate field on the Guide. Fill out/update your team member's Development Plan to reflect this conversation and agreements.

Step 8: On the second page of the Guide, ask your team member to select and check off which of the three options in the first/left column best describes their Feeling style, their Thinking style, and their Action style. Reveal to them which ones you chose for yourself and check those three options on the right column.

Step 9: In the Interpersonal Focus section, ask your team member to RANK ORDER the way they normally approach social/group interactions. In which order do they focus on their own needs first (personal comfort, safety, etc.), get a read and feel for the power structure in the room and with which group they want to interact, or identify one specific person they want to talk to, then move onto another specific person, then another. Mark the rank ordering for them in the first/left column, and share your own rank order in the right column.

Step 10: In the Communications Style section, ask your team member to RANK ORDER how they like to be communicated with. In which order of preference do they want a brief, executive summary of the situation, versus wanting to feel included and involved, versus feeling like they are cared for, versus wanting to know all the minutia of all the details so they have the full story. Document the rank order on the Guide. Share your rank order of preference in being communicated with.

Step 11: Review the commonalities and differences in each section and discuss them together. Identify and agree on how you will support each other in your differences, and even how you might remind each other to adopt different styles or perspectives (which may or may not be your top preferences or considerations) to be more effective in different situations. Include how you will address and provide feedback to each other if/when these Explicit Expectations are not being met. Document these in the Agreements field on the Guide.

Step 12: Maintain, review, and update this Guide with your team member on a regular basis (monthly? Quarterly? Semi-annually?) based on what is going on for you, your team member, and the organization. This will ensure that your mutual Explicit Expectations are being considered and met.

Rinse. Repeat: Do this for/with each of your team members, your manager, and key stakeholders to ensure everyone is aligned on each of your Explicit Expectations of each other.

EXPLICIT EXPECTATIONS ENGAGEMENT & ALIGNMENT GUIDE

[to be completed/reviewed/updated at least quarterly or whenever corporate directional changes occur, whichever comes first]

Our vision:

Our mission:

Our values:

Our goals and focus for the next year:

Our team's goals and focus for this quarter:

Our team's goals and focus for this month:

How often and when we'll meet for 1:1s/check-ins:

How, from who, and when will performance feedback be collected and shared?

> [   ]

What does recognition for a good job look like for you? How do you prefer to receive this?

> [   ]

Team member's career aspirations and timeframe (link to Development Plan):

> [   ]

	TEAM MEMBER	MANAGER
FEELING STYLE (PICK ONE)	☐ Focused on intuitively knowing what others need and helping them ☐ Pushing down feelings in favor of meeting goals and looking good ☐ Taking in own and others' feelings and seeking genuine and deep connection and being understood	☐ Focused on intuitively knowing what others need and helping them ☐ Pushing down feelings in favor of meeting goals and looking good ☐ Taking in own and others' feelings and seeking genuine and deep connection and being understood
THINKING STYLE (PICK ONE)	☐ Objectively collecting data and evidence to create mental models that predict what may happen so I am prepared and don't look foolish ☐ Seeking out dangers and what could go wrong/worst-case scenario so that I can prepare back-up and contingency plans to put into effect to be safe, comfortable, and secure ☐ Positively reframing and seeking out and taking advantage of opportunities and options	☐ Objectively collecting data and evidence to create mental models that predict what may happen so I am prepared and don't look foolish ☐ Seeking out dangers and what could go wrong/worst-case scenario so that I can prepare back-up and contingency plans to put into effect to be safe, comfortable, and secure ☐ Positively reframing and seeking out and taking advantage of opportunities and options
ACTION STYLE (PICK ONE)	☐ Immediate execution over that which I have power, control, and authority, seeking to protect my scope and people ☐ Stepping back first to gain a better understanding of the system implications and not wanting to cause any conflict ☐ Doing the right thing according to my values, morals, and ethics	☐ Immediate execution over that which I have power, control, and authority, seeking to protect my scope and people ☐ Stepping back first to gain a better understanding of the system implications and not wanting to cause any conflict ☐ Doing the right thing according to my values, morals, and ethics

		TEAM MEMBER	MANAGER
INTER-PERSONAL FOCUS (RANK ORDER)		☐ Self-Preservation: Own needs first	☐ Self-Preservation: Own needs first
		☐ 1:1: Intense one-on-one focus	☐ 1:1: Intense one-on-one focus
		☐ Social: Group Dynamics, Reading the Room	☐ Social: Group Dynamics, Reading the Room
COMMUNICATION STYLE (Rank order)		☐ Be brief/summarize, be bright, be gone	☐ Be brief/summarize, be bright, be gone
		☐ Involve/include me	☐ Involve/include me
		☐ Show me that you care about me	☐ Show me that you care about me
		☐ Give me all the details	☐ Give me all the details

AGREEMENTS BASED ON INSIGHTS FROM THE ABOVE STYLE EXERCISE:

- *Coach Me! Your Personal Board of Directors: Leadership Advice from the World's Greatest Coaches* by Brian Underhill, Jonathan Passmore, and Marshall Goldsmith (Eds.)
- *Coaching for Performance: The Principles and Practice of Coaching and Leadership* by Sir John Whitmore
- *Development Sequence in Small Groups* by Bruce Tuckman
- *Emotions of Normal People* by William Moulton Marston
- *The Energy of Success: Power Up Your Productivity, Transform Your Habits, and Maximize Workplace Motivation* by Rebecca Ahmed
- *Fierce Conversations: Achieving Success at Work and Life One Conversation at a Time* by Susan Scott
- *The First 90 Days: Proven Strategies for Getting Up to Speed Faster and Smarter* by Michael D. Watkins
- *First Things First: To Live, to Love, to Learn, to Leave a Legacy* by Stephen Covey, A. Roger Merrill, and Rebecca R. Merrill
- *A Guide to the Project Management Body of Knowledge (PMBOK Guide), 7th Edition* by the Project Management Institute
- *Good to Great: Why Some Companies Make the Leap … And Others Don't* by Jim Collins
- *Hello Stay Interviews, Goodbye Talent Loss* by Dr. Beverly Kaye and Sharon Jordan-Evans

- *Help them Grow or Watch them Go: Career Conversations Organizations Need and Employees Want* by Dr. Beverly Kaye & Julie Winkle Giulioni
- *The How and Why: Taking Care of Business with the Enneagram* by R. Karl Hebenstreit, Ph.D.
- *Leadership That Gets Results* by Daniel Goleman
- *Love 'Em or Lose 'Em: Getting Good People to Stay* by Dr. Beverly Kaye and Sharon Jordan-Evans
- *Leadership and the One Minute Manager: A Situational Approach to Leading Others* by Ken Blanchard, Patricia Zigarmi, and Drea Zigarmi
- *The Leadership Challenge (7th Edition): How to Make Extraordinary Things Happen in Organizations* by James Kouzes & Barry Posner
- *Management of Organizational Behavior: Utilizing Human Resources* by Paul Hersey and Ken Blanchard
- *Mastering Leadership: An Integrated Framework for Breakthrough Performance and Extraordinary Business Results* by Robert J. Anderson & William A. Adams
- *Organization Design* by Jay Galbraith
- *Scaling Leadership: Building Organizational Capability and Capacity to Create Outcomes that Matter Most* by Robert J. Anderson & William A. Adams
- *Start with Why: How Great Leaders Inspire Everyone to Take Action* by Simon Sinek
- *The Startup Owner's Manual: The Step-By-Step Guide for Building a Great Company* by Steve Blank & Bob Dorf
- *Transitions: Making Sense of Life's Changes* by William Bridges
- *Up Is Not the Only Way: Rethinking Career Mobility* by Dr. Beverly Kaye, Lindy Williams, and Lynn Cowart
- *What Got You Here Won't Get You There: How Successful People Become Even More Successful* by Marshall Goldsmith and Mark Reiter

Check out:
www.explicit-expectations.com
and
www.performandfunction.com
for updates on and resources related to
*Explicit Expectations: The Essential Guide
& Toolkit of Management Fundamentals*, including:

- A downloadable copy of the *Explicit Expectations Engagement & Alignment Guide*
- An AI-powered self-paced training course and coach based on this material

Made in the USA
Las Vegas, NV
06 August 2024

93454390R00079